WORK JUST GETS IN THE WAY OF MAKING MONEY

SCOTT JELINEK

WORK JUST GETS IN THE WAY OF MAKING MONEY

SIMPLE PROSPERITY THROUGH Real Estate Investing

Published by Advantage, Charleston, South Carolina.
Member of Advantage Media Group.

ADVANTAGE is a registered trademark and the Advantage colophon is a trademark of Advantage Media Group, Inc.

Printed in the United States of America.

ISBN: 978-1-59932-767-9
LCCN: 2016954048

Cover design by Katie Biondo.

This publication is designed to provide accurate and authoritative information in regard to the subject matter covered. It is sold with the understanding that the publisher is not engaged in rendering legal, accounting, or other professional services. If legal advice or other expert assistance is required, the services of a competent professional person should be sought.

Advantage Media Group is proud to be a part of the Tree Neutral® program. Tree Neutral offsets the number of trees consumed in the production and printing of this book by taking proactive steps such as planting trees in direct proportion to the number of trees used to print books. To learn more about Tree Neutral, please visit **www.treeneutral.com.**

Advantage Media Group is a publisher of business, self-improvement, and professional development books. We help entrepreneurs, business leaders, and professionals share their Stories, Passion, and Knowledge to help others Learn & Grow. Do you have a manuscript or book idea that you would like us to consider for publishing? Please visit **advantagefamily.com** or call **1.866.775.1696.**

To my wife, Lisa, and my son, Vince.

TABLE OF CONTENTS

ACKNOWLEDGMENTS

I would like to express my deepest gratitude to the people who have helped me to get where I am today and for many of the ideas presented in this book.

- To Lisa Ann Jelinek, my wife and partner, for allowing me to be who I am and always keeping our business and family on a steady course.

- To Arlene Jelinek, my mother, for always supporting my ideas and new ventures.

- To Stacy Chianese, for working side by side with me for many years and keeping me moving in the right direction.

- To Kevin Gilbert, the original apprentice, my partner and friend for rolling the dice with me on every new idea and never giving up.

- To the Entrepreneurs' Organization (EO) and especially Forum Three, for acting as a sounding board and reminding me that I am not alone on this crazy roller coaster.

- To James E. Dilley and Thomas Dobson, for being my friends and mentors, having taught me more about real estate and about life than I could have ever hoped for.

 INTRODUCTION

TAKE CONTROL OF YOUR FINANCIAL FUTURE

Would you like to get out of the rat race? Are you ready to start cashing checks for $25,000, $50,000, or more? If you follow my step-by-step action plan, you can do just that as a successful real estate investor. This is not a get-rich-quick scheme, and I'm not promising something for nothing. To be successful in real estate, you will have to work, study, and learn the systems that I present here, but you don't need to be a genius or have a big bank account. All you need is persistence, hard work, and a desire to learn. I am so confident that anyone who learns my systems and applies them will be cashing big checks that I will give a $100,000 guarantee.

MY GUARANTEE

I guarantee that if you follow the systems in this book, even on a part-time basis while working your regular job, you will make a minimum of $100,000 over the next twelve months.

If you don't, I'll refund the purchase price of this book, plus the cost of shipping and handling.

Now that I've gotten that out of the way, I should tell you that writing is not what I do. I am a full-time real estate investor. I have been investing in real estate since 1994, but I didn't always do it full time. I dabbled in real estate for many years, wasted lots of time, and made many mistakes before I hit on the winning strategies I present here. I wish I'd had a book like this starting out—or even some years into my real estate career. It would have saved me an immense amount of time and money. I am writing this book so that you can learn from my mistakes and eventual success and take the fastest possible route to making money in real estate. This applies equally to young entrepreneurs just starting out and older folks trying to correct what they've done wrong for the last forty years.

Since the age of sixteen, I have read hundreds of books about business and real estate, and though I learned a lot, none of them presented the complete picture that I'll give you in these pages. In fact, what you are about to learn goes against the principles most books promote. The reason is simple: the truth is not sexy and doesn't sell nearly as well as the latest thirty-day plan to making millions. Instead of a scheme like that, I'm offering you reality, the reality that I wish I had grasped from day one. I have tried other approaches, and the conventional ones that promise easy money fail—partly because they dupe you into seeing money as the goal. It's not. The goal is freedom. Money is merely the ticket to freedom. Real estate happens to be my chosen means of making money, but to be truly successful—and happy—we must keep the real goal in our sights, continually adjusting our approach to aim for it and not simply for more money.

Most of the people out there teaching get-rich-quick schemes and running investment seminars are not really investors. The high roller who travels the country fifty-one weeks a year telling people that he buys houses every day probably makes his money selling courses, not doing deals. Some of these guys probably haven't done a deal in so long that their only knowledge of the rapidly changing market comes from what they see on television. I, on the other hand, invest full time. What does this mean? Well, when I wake up in the morning, I go to my office and spend my day looking for new deals and working on the ones I have in progress. This book teaches you the same exact techniques for investing that I use day in and day out. It is, I believe, the best starting point for budding entrepreneurs, as well as for old pros who want some new tips and insights, because it offers a big-picture view of investing.

If you're serious about making money as a real estate investor, I recommend that you also take advantage of my course, the Master Investor Academy, at www.MasterInvestorAcademy.com. While this book will give the most comprehensive overview of real estate investing available, books are static. The online course is a good complement because it offers extensive videos on guerrilla marketing, phone scripts, the three-step buying process, and much more. The course video trainings are constantly updated, and joining the Academy gives you access to all future trainings for free. You also receive access to all my forms and contracts, as well as to limited coaching through the Master Investor Academy forum. I'll personally answer your questions in that forum and even help you work out the details of specific deals. This book provides you with the confidence and the knowledge base you need to become a real estate investor, and the Master Investor Academy course supplies many of the tools you'll need to get deals done, while keeping your techniques fresh.

This book is called *Work Just Gets in the Way of Making Money* because I can't count the number of times people have told me that the reason they can't invest or make better lives for themselves is that they're too busy working. All too often, when I am teaching people how to invest, they respond, "That's easy for you, you don't have a job. I'm too busy at work for this stuff." I wish they could hear themselves. It's precisely because they're busy at work—usually at jobs they don't like—that they should learn to invest. I love convincing friends and acquaintances of this and helping them break the chains that tie them to joyless jobs, but teaching people to become successful investors takes an enormous amount of time. I spent so much time helping friends and acquaintances, it eventually got in the way of my own investing. That's why I decided to write this book.

The techniques I show you here are simple. They don't require much money or risk. The strategies are basic, but you will have to put some time into learning the system. Education is vital to your success. You will have to learn everything you can about this business, and then learn some more. Never stop learning. The market is continually changing—that's one of the exciting things about real estate—so it's vital to think of yourself as a lifelong learner. I have spent tens of thousands of dollars on courses and seminars—I still do—and have never regretted it. This, again, is the advantage of my course, the Master Investor Academy—it's constantly updated and improved—but whether or not you take advantage of that course or choose others, it's important to keep honing your skills and building your strategies.

You are probably reading this book because you're sick and tired of your job. Perhaps you work harder than your bosses. You might be smarter than they are, too, but somehow they're the ones cashing big checks. If you have diplomas on the wall, those haven't helped, because even with the education that seemed like such a good invest-ment at the time, you just squeak by. Or maybe you're already an investor but could be doing better; you're looking for new ways to profit. Whichever of these scenarios describes you, I will take you to the goal step by step. You can end all of the struggling and scraping right now if you're willing to commit. I am not recommending that you quit your job (not yet anyway) but rather offering you a way to begin investing immediately—this week, tomorrow, or even today if you like.

Does that sound too soon? Not ready to take the plunge? Well, there's the problem. I will teach you concrete investing strategies here, but even more important, I will teach you a new way of thinking. You need to learn that you have the ability to go out and make serious money. You are in control, and the only thing holding you back—no offense—is you. You can't just sit around until Friday and hope that there's enough money to cover your bills or pray that your job will be there next week. I am going to show you how to make an average check of $25,000 (some will be much larger). Mustering the will and determination to do your first deal is key, not because of the money, but because once you cash that check you will have taken the biggest step in changing the way you think. You can only do this in your spare time? You can only do deals three or four times a year? Great. That's more than enough to change your life forever.

If you're like me, you'll get addicted the day you cash that first check. You will never look at money the same way again. When your boss offers you a fifteen-cent-an-hour raise or a $15,000 annual salary boost, you'll laugh and want to leave that dead-end job. It will be time to take complete control of your economic future and break the last chains limiting your earnings. Until then, I suggest you suck it up at work and begin by investing in real estate on evenings and weekends, whatever time you have off. That will be plenty. The checks will start coming in, and you'll realize that the upside potential is like nothing you've ever seen.

Much of what I'll discuss involves taking control of your own earnings and time. I still work hard, but when I wake up in the morning, I decide what my day will look like. If it's sunny out, I might decide to jet ski all day or sit by the pool. Whenever I sleep late, I tell my wife, "It's a good thing I don't have a job—I'd be fired within a week." Sad but true.

I didn't achieve this lifestyle or a sizeable income overnight. There are two ways to learn: from your own experiences and from others'. Let me tell you as someone who knows, learning from your own experiences becomes extremely costly and time consuming. Unfortunately, that's the route I took. I wish I hadn't. I wish that I'd known enough back then to know that I didn't know anything. For years, I struggled in challenging businesses of all sorts and dabbled in real estate. I didn't have any formal education, so I had to learn everything the hard way. Even within real estate, it took years of trial and error before I hit on the strategies that offer the highest profit for the lowest risk—with the fewest headaches. What I am offering you here is the benefit of all of my experiments and mistakes, countless wasted dollars, and many years in the school of hard knocks. This book will save you untold time and money and show you the fastest route to financial success.

I have provided a comprehensive overview of real estate investing here, and unlike many books, this one gives practical step-by-step advice to get you started right away (exactly what to say to buyers, how to approach sellers, how to calculate offers, etc.). As far as a return on your investment, it's much more valuable than a college degree. But if all you do is learn, then this education—like so many college degrees these days—will be useless. You must take action, plunge in, and do a deal. I will return to this theme again and again. If you wait until everything seems perfect, you'll never make a buck. You must do something every day that brings you closer to your goals. Watching *American Idol* doesn't count. This business is simple, but it's not easy. Learning and applying my systems will take time. That's why my guarantee says that you must *follow* the systems in the book and not just read about them. By buying this book, you have taken the first step. If you also can believe in yourself and act, you'll soon be enjoying a world where work just gets in the way.

# CHAPTER 1

REAL ESTATE SCOTT'S WAY

Before I impart my systems for real estate investing, I'd like to share with you a little bit about myself, how I got into real estate, and how my strategies evolved over many years. I was born in 1973 on Long Island in New York, the fourth of six children. Some people develop into entrepreneurs—I was born one. By the age of five, I had detailed plans for opening a restaurant, including professionally printed signs and menus (my father was a printer). Later, I made $20 to $30 a day selling candy in school—good money for a kid, though it came at the expense of learning in class. My brother and I mowed lawns during summer and shoveled snow all winter. I loved the snow, which taught me one of my first lessons about supply and demand, as well as how to build customer lists. Though shoveling was hard work, it often snowed again the day after I'd made my rounds. I could go right back to the same customers—skipping all the people that said no—and make my fee all over again. The work wasn't steady, but in a snowy week I could easily make $200 a day.

At the age of fifteen, I started my first legitimate business, a vending-machine route. I bought machines from BJ's Wholesale Club and placed them in local pizza shops. After building the business up, I eventually sold all the machines to the shop owners at a profit. I also worked at the kinds of businesses most teenagers do—gas station, stationery store, Orange Julius, shoe store. It was at one of these, a little hotdog stand in the mall, that I first saw a real entrepreneur at work, at close enough range to learn some valuable lessons. My boss owned several hot dog stands, but he did other things, too, whenever he saw an opportunity. At Christmastime, for instance, he set up kiosks in the mall to sell those premade cheese gift baskets. He always had his eye on the next angle. I loved his energy and resourcefulness, and fortunately he didn't mind teaching others.

One day at an employee party, admiring his massive house and full-sized arcade games (a big deal then), I saw that his sort of ingenuity and hustle could make for a pretty nice life. He was, I realized, the wealthiest guy I knew. The interesting thing to me was that all his wealth came from selling hot dogs. Not exactly a glamorous profession but apparently quite a profitable one, at least as he went at it. I was about seventeen then and working every hour I could. School did not interest me, but business sure did.

In 1990, a recruiter at the mall where I worked explained to me that you could join the army at seventeen with your parents' consent. Hungry to get out of the classroom and into the real world, I quit school in the eleventh grade and joined up. I served my time and returned eager for adventure and a way to make money. I quickly hit on one of the best hustles ever. My brother and I walked the beach, carrying a cooler and selling sodas. If you have ever been to Jones Beach in New York, you know why this was so profitable. The walk from the shoreline to anyplace you can buy a soda is enormous, so if you don't pack one, you'll happily pay $2 a can. The same can cost me twenty-five cents, so our profit margins were huge, about $200 a day on average. I was making money and having a great time doing it. Unfortunately, the more established entrepreneurs selling sodas on the beach weren't too happy about my new business. After several heated exchanges with other angry freelancers, I gave it up.

In 1992, I moved to Virginia Beach, hoping to sell sodas on the beaches there, but I quickly learned that legal vendors and nearby stores had the market covered. Instead, I began selling merchandise at local flea markets. I would buy faux name-brand sunglasses for $13 a dozen and sell them for $10 a pair. I bought all sorts of products in New York—pocketbooks, watches, DVDs, CDs, clothes—to stay ahead of the competition, who shipped in their merch. I drove mine back and had a great time selling it. The business thrived.

I had always been interested in real estate, but like most people, I thought I didn't have the kind of money, credit, or job necessary to buy property. I was nineteen and renting a townhouse with my sister for $675 a month when my brother brought me a flyer that changed my life. The page he'd found stuck in his front door advertised a townhouse for sale nearby. Anyone could buy this house for $5,000 down, according to the flyer. *No credit, no job? No problem!* This was a nonqualifying assumable mortgage. These arrangements disappeared in the late eighties, but they allowed anyone to take over a mortgage with no qualifying whatsoever—a great proposition for investors.

I made an appointment to see the house and tucked $5,000 in cash in my pocket. The owner gave me a tour, and I pretended to understand what I saw, when in reality everything I knew about real estate fit on that flyer.

After about five minutes of careful consideration, during which I tried to look as thoughtful and wise as a nineteen-year-old can, I pulled out my five grand and said, "I'll take it." I figured I would hand her the money, and she would turn over the keys.

"Hold on," she said, no doubt suppressing a smile. "We need to write a contract and have a closing."

This was my first lesson in real estate. The second lesson was that "$5,000 down" isn't actually $5,000. After closing costs, insurance, title policy, and other expenses, my total came to about $7,000. I scrounged up the money and closed on my first house. The payment was about the same as my $675 rent, only now I was an owner. (I still own that house, and today it rents for $1,275.)

My flea market business was doing well. Unfortunately, like selling sodas on the beach, this endeavor wasn't strictly legal. After some run-ins with the law, I decided to make a change. For my first legitimate business in Virginia, I turned to the same field that so many entrepreneurs do early in their careers—landscaping. The start-up costs are next to nothing, and demand is always present, which is why, I think, so many budding businesspeople give this a go early on. To this day, I constantly refer to my landscaping days whenever someone complains about not having money or a job. Grab a lawnmower and knock on some doors, I tell them, and you can easily make a hundred bucks a day. I charged just $10 to mow townhouse lawns—not a fortune, but they were small and easy to cut.

As I drove my landscaping route, I called the number on every sign I saw advertising a home for sale. I was curious to see if I'd gotten a good deal on my house, since I hadn't done any research before buying it—and I was curious about the real estate industry in general. Calling on for-sale signs is a great habit even if you have no intention of buying. It gives you a feel for values and what's happening in your market. The Internet is an incredible tool for real estate, but there's no substitute for seeing a house in person.

One day, I called the number of a for-sale sign on my block, and the owner told me that I could have it for $2,000 down if I took over her mortgage. This house was identical to mine and in the same location—another nonqualifying mortgage assumption. The price ticked me off. I must have overpaid for mine, I thought, because this one cost only $2,000 down, less than half the $5,000 I'd shelled out. Pretty soon, though, I was contemplating a purchase. *I must be crazy for even considering this*, I thought. I had no money and just paying for the house I lived in was a struggle.

Before long, though, I'd scraped the money together and bought my second house, reasoning that if I averaged the down payments on the two properties, I'd be doing pretty well. By that logic, it seemed foolish not to buy. I was starting to think like an investor—a completely naïve and inexperienced one, but still, I'd been bitten hard by the real estate bug. That second house triggered dreams of empire. I loved the idea that I could borrow money and tenants would pay it back. Genius! If I kept acquiring houses, I'd be filthy rich in time, with dozens of properties.

I quickly found a tenant for the second house. I would barely break even on the rent, but so what? I could tread water, and the house would pay for itself over time. That same year, I bought another house, this one for only $500 down. The owner, who lived out of town, couldn't do the deal until she removed the homeless guy squatting in the house, so I offered to help. With no knowledge of the law or the Landlord Tenant Act, I put his belongings on the driveway, changed the locks, and left a note on the door. I had no idea what I was I doing, but I'd learned how to scout an area, find a house I could buy, purchase it, and rent it out. What more did I need to know?

My McDonald's Plan was born. This was what I called my real estate investing system, which was the kind of strategy only a high school dropout could dream up. My first couple of houses were worth about $65,000 (about $169,000 today). If I bought a million dollars' worth of property (about fifteen houses), I reasoned, then I could get a job at McDonald's if I wanted and simply wait. This is no sleight against McDonald's, which has a great business model. The point is, it wouldn't matter how big my checks were or where I worked. I'd be paying off those fifteen mortgages year after year, and in time, I'd be a millionaire.

While keeping an eye out for houses, I continued landscaping for more than two years until it wore me out. When that point finally came, I sold the business for a whopping $5,000. I used that money as the down payment on a limousine. I didn't know anything about limos except that I liked them and driving one seemed like much cleaner work than landscaping. If you're sensing a pattern here, you've got the young Scott Jelinek pegged. I was ambitious, energetic, fearless, and thoroughly green. I believed in leaping first and looking later, and I knew of only one way to learn—the hard way (this book presents a much easier method).

At first, I just parked the limo in my driveway and answered incoming calls on my cell phone. My payment on the vehicle came to just $333 a month. The car was older, but I charged less than my competitors. I only advertised with business cards, flyers, and the occasional classified ad, but the business went well enough that I bought a second car and parked it at home, too. My brother and brother-in-law drove for me, and the money rolled in. I used some of it to put an ad in the Yellow Pages. My phone started ringing the second the phonebook came out and didn't stop for years. Soon, I had an office, six limos, full-time advertising campaign, secretary, phone lines, fax lines, and credit card machines. For the first time, I had all the trappings of a serious business, but the work was no longer fun. I brought in more money than ever, around $40,000 a month, and didn't make a dime. I was spinning my wheels—pun intended—with all of that overhead, the car payments, and insurance.

This was my first taste of a lesson that took many years to sink in, one I'll emphasize again and again in this book. Success in business isn't measured by the size of the operation, the volume of dollars changing hands, the number of limos you put on the road, or the number of rental homes you control. The amount of money coming in must be larger than the amount going out. Period. Lots of successful people in business, especially these days, have no office at all and little or no overhead. Others with impressive offices and sizable portfolios are barely scraping by. Another lesson I learned from the limo business involved how little I knew when I started out. After two years running the operation, I bought a book on how to start a limousine company from *Entrepreneur* magazine. It maintained that the minimum capital required to start such a business was $250,000.

I was counting more headaches than profits and wasn't sure what to do next when one of my drivers offered me $150,000 for the business. Sold. Paying off my debts left only about $50,000 from the proceeds, but at least I was out.

Next, I bought a tanning salon—a terrible business, with long hours, frequent problems, and low profit potential. Of course, I also discovered all of this the hard way. While painting the place prior to opening, I stumbled onto a nearby sub sandwich shop that the owner offered to sell me for $2,500. I couldn't believe it. It turned out he had just built a new store nearby in a brand new shopping center. He wanted to close this location but was tied to the lease. I told my mother about the offer, expecting her to talk some sense into me, but instead she said, "You have to take it at that price. It's a score!" I ran the sub shop for about three months before selling it for $25,000.

I sold the tanning salon shortly after that. Running these establishments was tough—much tougher than I remembered my first attempts at business as a kid. The whole time I was starting, buying, and selling various small businesses, I worked real estate on the side, but it never occurred to me that I might have less risk, fewer headaches, and bigger profits if I made that my main business. My tunnel vision stemmed from the fact that I didn't have a strategy beyond the McDonald's Plan: buy a home, rent it out at a price that covered the mortgage (barely), and act as a traditional landlord. The payoff from these real estate deals would take thirty years, but I was well on my way.

I had gotten up to ten houses when I sold the tanning salon and sub shop, and around the same time I hit three major snags: repairs, repairs, and repairs. With ten houses to take care of, it seemed that someone called me with a problem nearly every day. Sometimes I only had to fix a small leak under a sink, and sometimes I had to replace a heating system or an entire roof. I was barely breaking even on the rents and had no cash left over for repairs or vacancies. My dream of doing nothing for thirty years, besides watching equity grow, was fading fast. Before long, the repairs took so much time, energy, and money that I considered getting out of real estate altogether.

I was close to quitting when I had lunch with a friend who also invested in real estate. That lunch became another life changer (here's part of why I encourage you to hang around with other investors, advice I'll return to later). My friend introduced me to lease options, a simple concept but one I'd never heard of. A lease option allows you to lease a house to an end user, who has the option to buy it within a certain time frame. The odds are quite good that the people leasing won't buy, but—and here is the part that changed my life— the tenants are responsible for repairs while they're in the house. This one change eliminated a massive number of headaches and opened up a world of opportunity. Now, I could buy as many properties as I wanted. The McDonald's Plan moved to a fast track!

Of course, the McDonald's Plan required another business to pay the bills, and one always seemed to fall in my path. The next opportunity popped up when the woman I'd bought the tanning salon from called me about the bar she was working at, a place in the same shopping center. Its three owners were feuding, and one, who owned half the business, wanted to sell. I met with him, and before I knew it, I was in the bar business. The seller didn't mention our transaction to his partners, so let's just say that introducing myself to them was more than a little awkward. Within three months, though, I'd bought them out and was the sole owner of Krossroads, a cozy local tavern in Virginia Beach.

Running a bar is another world, and as usual, I had to learn a lot in a short period of time. I didn't have enough experience to make sure that the corporation was clean, so discovering that I was now responsible for a bunch of old debts and unpaid taxes came as a shock—more tuition paid to the school of hard knocks. Still, I rolled up my sleeves and learned yet another difficult business. In fact, I started dreaming about a national chain and during the next eighteen months acquired two more bars.

Operating this business, however, didn't just prove difficult—it changed who I was. Did I have fun? Of course, but I also hung out in a bar every day and drank and smoked every day—and that came to seem perfectly normal. Here I learned yet another lesson at the school of hard knocks, one I touched on previously and will return to later in the book. You've probably heard the saying that you are the average of the five people you hang out with most. This adage is absolutely true. If you want to become a successful real estate investor, you must start hanging around other real estate investors. At the bar, I socialized with people who drank every day. They had working class jobs and spent $30 to $50 a day drinking but couldn't afford basic needs or to keep their homes out of foreclosure. They wouldn't dream of skipping the bar. After two years of making this my circle, I'd had enough.

After I sold the bars, I owned and ran many more businesses—a barter company (which I sold for five times my purchase price), a hot dog shop, several local newspapers, a property management company, a large vending route, an oceanfront gift shop, several restaurants, and others. Each year, though, I also learned more about real estate—all of it the hard way—and expanded my property holdings. I read books, attended seminars, bought and sold homes, experimented. The three common principles all the gurus seemed to agree on were: leverage, leverage, and leverage. This, they said, was *the* key to getting ahead in real estate, and I became such an avid disciple that I altered the McDonald's Plan. I refinanced my properties and used all of the proceeds to purchase more houses. It seemed like a great idea at the time. I amassed eighty-four properties on the way to my new goal of one hundred, and I had nearly $1 million in cash. I was doing exactly what the experts recommended, and it was working.

Until it wasn't.

In 2007, as the real estate market was crashing hard, my income suddenly dried up. Overnight, I lost millions in equity. Everything I'd learned in all those books and at endless seminars went up in smoke, along with my plans. Gradually, I spent every dime I had in the struggle of my life, just trying to hold on. The money ran out, and I fell behind on mortgage payments. The disaster was compounded during the Great Recession because not only was my business floundering but so were most of my tenants' incomes. I had more defaults and delinquent payers than ever, just when I could least afford them. Some of my houses went into foreclosure. It's difficult to convey just how hard this was. I was the guy who stopped foreclosures and bought houses—but now I was on the other side of the equation.

Eventually I lost about fifty of my properties to foreclosure, but I never quit. I never gave up, and today I have rebuilt a portfolio of nearly seventy rentals—only this time I'm playing a very different ball game. I do not follow the leverage model anymore. The housing crash created a new world, and I responded with a new way of doing real estate. As awful as the Great Recession was, I wouldn't trade the experience for anything. It completely changed my way of thinking and helped me to rebuild my business on an unshakable foundation. Chicago became a better city after the Great Chicago Fire, and to this day it has some of the toughest fire codes in the country. Architects in San Francisco design with earthquakes in mind, and their structures are better because of past disasters.

I reengineered my business in the same way, to eliminate as much risk as possible, and I'll share this hard-won strategy with you in the coming chapters. My systems will differ significantly from the strategies of other "experts," who still preach the gospel of leverage. How short their memories are. Here is the plain, boring, commonsense truth about my experience in the housing crash. Before the boom, I had around twenty good rentals. If I hadn't gotten caught up in the boom and hadn't listened to the language of leverage, I would have had those properties free and clear. All I had to do was . . . nothing.

Perhaps now you can see why so many gurus still tout leverage as *the* way to make a large amount of money in a small amount of time. Their approach is sexy. It conjures images of fancy cars, lavish mansions, and a fast track to millions. My strategy, which insists that you keep debt to a minimum and repay loans as quickly as you can, is much less flashy. People want to hear that they can immediately start living the lifestyle they've always dreamed of, and many will happily pay for any book or seminar that makes that sort of promise. Parts of the gospel according to Scott are much less palatable—for example: you *must* live within your means to achieve financial success, and it's better to have a beater that's paid for than a Beamer that the bank owns.

Don't get me wrong—there is a serious upside here. Remember my guarantee: if you learn and follow my systems, you can make at least $100,000 in the next year by investing in real estate part time. But I'll teach you to minimize your risk as you invest, rather than encourage you to expose yourself while striving for a million bucks right out of the gate. I'll remind you of the unsexy truth that earning $100,000 in the next twelve months will be meaningless if you spend $105,000.

I have bought, sold, and run endless businesses. Some of them did very well, and some flopped. I spent considerable space in this chapter detailing my vast and varied business ventures to make this point: after all of the things I've tried, there's nothing I would rather do than invest in real estate. I believe that no business is easier to enter or has a better upside, lower risk, or fewer headaches than real estate the way I do it. It took me many years to realize that this is my avocation, and it took many more to hit on the strategies that get the best results and are effective in any market. It is partly because my learning curve was so long and partly because I didn't have much formal education that I felt inspired to write this book. I grabbed every scrap of knowledge I could over the years from various books, seminars, and courses, as well as from friends and associates. Those sources proved invaluable, and I still think of myself as a student. I'm always buying real estate books, and I attend a seminar at least once a year.

Assembling the knowledge I now have, however, was difficult. One good book that provided both the big picture of real estate investing and the nitty-gritty detail of how to get deals done would have saved me massive amounts of time, stress, and money. I did it the hard way, and I wrote this book so that you won't have to.

the wall. Nobody mentions that while college no longer guarantees a good job, it does guarantee major debt just when you're trying to get life started. While you're worrying about how to make ends meet, hooray, shiny new credit cards arrive in the mail! They ease the short-term pressure. What about the long term? Forget about the long term! Now that you have your diploma, surely you deserve a new car? No one with a degree like yours should have to drive that old clunker! So what if you don't have a job yet. You can always work retail for a couple months until your ship comes in.

Sound familiar? This is all it takes to get on the hamster wheel and remain there *for life,* because once you're on it, the pace only increases. Don't worry, you'll get a raise soon and everything will be okay. Then comes marriage and kids. A house and diapers. No, it's not going to be okay. It's not set up to be okay. The system is designed to give you just enough to survive and not a penny more. You are on the fifty-ninth payment of a five-year loan on your Beamer? Whew, almost free of one debt! But all of your friends just bought the new model, and besides, yours has a hundred thousand miles on it. Surely you deserve the new one? You work hard. You make more money than half of those friends, so why shouldn't you? So you do.

What you don't realize is that every time you sign on the dotted line, you are signing away more of your freedom, more of your life. Now, please don't get me wrong. I am not saying that you shouldn't have nice things. Nice things are fine, but you can't get them this way. This way, the nice things are never really yours—they belong to creditors.

Before I got reeducated, I was bringing in about $30,000 a month from flipping properties. I owned about eighty rentals and was, by all accounts, quite successful. No one knew that, under the glittery surface, I was drowning in debt. It was killing me. I would make a pile of cash one day and use it to fill a hole the next. Two major events changed my approach—meeting a man who bought one of my rental properties and living through the real estate bust of 2007.

It was 2005, and I was rolling in cash (everyone in real estate was that year). I had a rental home for sale and a buyer lined up for it. The buyer asked me to meet him at a Starbucks to go over the paperwork. When he walked in, I could tell he was a regular. Everyone knew him, and the barista had his drink ready before he reached the counter. When we got to talking, I learned that he had ten rentals and did about four flips a year. *Ha, chump change,* I thought. I boasted about my eighty rentals and the fifty to sixty flips I did annually. He was a small fry compared to me, but he had an air I couldn't quite figure. He exuded security and confidence. He seemed successful in some intangible way. Despite his small-time operation, time didn't appear to worry him, and he never looked stressed. He looked, well, free.

After that deal, we stayed in touch and met regularly at that Starbucks for coffee. What I learned from him would change me forever. He only had ten or eleven rentals, but all of them were owned free and clear. He only brought in about $11,000 a month, but of that, he took home about $9,000 after taxes, insurance, and repairs. I brought in about $80,000 a month but had eighty mortgages. I had to do deals and make excess cash to feed the beast. He did just four flips a year, making about $120,000 total, and brought it all home. I grossed $70,000 to $100,000 a month, but with all of my overhead, I brought home $25,000 or $30,000 at best. My overhead costs always stayed the same, so if I had one bad month, I'd spend several more recovering from it, scraping by and digging myself out.

The more interesting part of my new friend's approach, however, was that utilities and food comprised his total domestic expenses.

He had no mortgage; he owned his house free and clear. He had no car payments and no credit cards. He spoke of those things as the devils they are, though I'd never seen them that way. Big picture? He brought home about $200,000 annually, and his living expenses totaled $25,000 a year. Wow! That blew my mind. While I was boasting about my success and pegging him for small potatoes, he must have been shaking his head in pity. He was the successful one, and his greatest asset was freedom. If he didn't flip a single property, he was fine. If he had three vacancies or major repairs, he was fine. If he decided he didn't want to work this month—or this year, for that matter—fine.

Meeting him changed my outlook. For years, I had been chasing a dollar amount: $100,000 a month. This was what I thought I needed to be successful. What a chump! That kind of goal gets you into a zero-sum game. I had years in which I made a boatload of money, but my expenses were always a boatload plus one. I bought into the scam that tells us money is the goal and resisted the true goal of freedom. I wanted to change after I learned my new friend's philosophy, but I kept falling back on the arguments that countless real estate books and seminars had engrained in me. Their biggest argument was the one I mentioned in the first chapter—the gospel of leverage.

Many readers have probably heard this example or one like it: if you have $100,000, you can buy one house free and clear, or you can buy ten houses by putting $10,000 down on each. If homes rise in value by 10 percent, the first approach gives you a return of 10 percent, but the second example yields a return of 100 percent. Leverage makes perfect sense—until you get burned. Even Robert Kiyosaki's book *Rich Dad Poor Dad*, a book I love, promotes buying cash-producing assets, financing the thing you want, and then using the cash those assets produce to pay the debt. The ideas that rest on leverage always seem great, sometimes even brilliant. I truly believed in and defended them. I remember at times thinking, sure, my Starbucks friend seems relaxed and he has some security, but if he really knew what he was doing, he would make a killing. He could easily leverage the properties he owned into many more, and all of them would produce income and build equity. This was my thinking before the second event that changed my outlook forever—the real estate crash of 2007.

Before the Great Recession, I believed I was on the right path, and then my flipping business ended overnight, because suddenly no one could get a mortgage. Wholesaling houses (a strategy we'll discuss later) died because my investors couldn't sell the properties they had. My rental business suffered major increases in late payments and evictions. As I mentioned in the last chapter, I lost fifty properties, spending nearly $1 million during the next couple of years, trying to carry the debt and hold onto what I'd built.

I thought I was a high roller and looked down on my friend from Starbucks, when in reality I was the one stuck on the hamster wheel, forced to run faster and faster just to stay alive. It took the disaster of the housing crash to make me realize where I stood and to make this principle crystal clear: all debt is bad. Yes, even "good debt" is bad, and you can't be *free* until you're *debt-free*.

The strategies that encourage big leverage rest on the idea that money is the goal, which is why it's vital to recognize that freedom is what you're really after. Once I realized this, I salvaged what I could from the crash and rebuilt a solid business. I no longer chase overhead. All of my cars are owned free and clear. I don't own my house free and clear yet, but I'm on a short-term plan to get there. I have eliminated most of my monthly obligations, and I'm working

CHAPTER 2: GET A LIFE

on the rest. I only wish I had known to operate this way—and to keep my sights on the real goal—when I was starting out. Why? Well, by getting off the hamster wheel, avoiding debt, and staying focused on the true goal, I've reached a place where I can vacation at least twelve weeks a year. I work hard some days, and on others I lay by the pool. If the market tanks, I'll be just fine. I have everything I want, but I live within my means. If this sounds a lot like our friend from Starbucks, you've got the idea.

You can do the same thing. I'll show you how in the coming chapters. If you're just starting out, you're lucky. You have a chance to do it right from the beginning. If you're older and already dragged down by the chains of debt and overhead as I was, don't worry. Yours will be a longer and more challenging journey, but you definitely can get there. Take comfort from the fact that you would not be able to appreciate the peace you'll eventually find without the preceding struggle.

There are three steps to achieving freedom, and you must follow them in order. They require some sacrifices in the beginning, but if you stick to the plan and break free, you'll realize that the alternative requires a much greater sacrifice—your life. Whenever you sign on that dotted line, you are agreeing now to work later in order to pay the interest on whatever you purchased. With each purchase, your life gets harder, and the hamster wheel spins faster. It's an insidious, slippery slope. Eventually, you'll find yourself working just for interest payments. At one point, my credit card interest alone was about $5,000 a month. That was just the *interest*. I was enslaved. And for what? Things? They weren't worth trading my life for.

THREE STEPS TO FREEDOM

Before we detail the three steps to freedom, you need to know why you are doing this. What do you want? What's your vision? When I ask people what they want, the answer is usually "more money" or "more things," and occasionally it is "more time" or even "freedom." Realizing that freedom is the goal, however, is only the beginning. When we dig deeper, most people do not know what they would do if they were free. I no longer need to do deals just to survive; I can honestly say that I love flipping houses, coaching, and changing people's lives. I will continue to do this work regardless of how much money I have or need.

What would you do if you were completely free? It's an important question because this is what you're working toward. This is the goal. Who do you want to be? What do you want your days to look like? If you won $100 million tomorrow, what would you do with the rest of your life? Most people don't know. Their identities are too tied to their work, and they've been too busy to consider the question. I'm asking you to think hard about it. Once you know the answer, you'll probably realize you don't need anywhere near $100 million; odds are, you can make that vision happen for a fraction of what you thought it would take.

I want you now to take a few minutes, grab a sheet of paper and a pen. Close your eyes—yes, I'm serious, close them!—and try to envision your ideal future. Forget about mansions and Lamborghinis for now. I'm not saying you can't have those things, only that lavish possessions aren't the purpose of this exercise. Instead, envision your perfect day. How would you like your morning to go? Where would you spend it, with whom, doing what? If you don't like the work you do now—most people don't—what sort of work would you like to do? On what terms? Do you picture yourself in an office with your own staff, wheeling and dealing; putting in time with a laptop and cell phone at the cozy coffee shop on the corner; or avoiding work as completely as possible? Do you imagine yourself planning trips and traveling to exotic locales, playing piano four hours a day, training for a marathon, or owning a restaurant?

Whatever you imagine, write it down. Nothing is too weird or unlikely. You must have a vision before you can work on the steps that will make it a reality. This mental exercise is important because once the vision is clear, it makes all future decisions easy. Always choose the thing that brings you closer to your vision, no matter how much easier it might seem to avoid that choice, no matter what the payoff for putting it off might be. It's a cliché, but any day could be your last. Stop delaying. "Someday" never comes!

Once you have your vision clearly in mind, you're ready to take the three steps that will make it a reality.

Step One: Live At or Below Your Means

I can already hear you yelling, wherever you are. You didn't buy this book for advice on how to clip coupons and drive a hoopty. I get it, but don't worry—living "within your means" won't always mean living frugally. This step is only tough in the beginning, when your means are limited. Implementing this iron rule and always sticking to it is what sets the stage for your means to increase. Once they do, you can get all those things you want and more. Freedom. I say that you must "always" stick to this rule because even when you dramatically boost your income—as I guarantee you will if you follow my systems—you will have to make sure that you don't spend more than you make.

You can make $300,000 a year, and if your lifestyle requires $300,001, you are flat broke, working as much as you can just to survive. You might be surviving in a nicer house, with a nicer car, but at what cost? You would be better off making just $50,000 a year and living a lifestyle that requires $30,000. It can be difficult, but this is the way you must learn to think.

In step one, painful as it might be, I want you to sell anything you make payments on. Now, I cheated on this step and refused to sell my house. My wife and I love our home and so I decided to work on paying it off instead of moving into a place I could pay cash for. There's my confession—but I got rid of everything else I made payments on, and so must you. Sell the jet skis, the boat, the vacation house in the mountains (which you hardly use anyway because you're too busy working to make the mortgage payments).

The idea here is to make the number of dollars you require to survive as low as possible. At one point, I "needed" $30,000 a month to survive. What the hell was I thinking? One bad month would set in motion a snowball effect that could last years, and for what? Stuff. Trust me when I tell you that all of this *stuff*, the bling you think you need to keep up with the neighbors, is just a chain around your ankles. Again, before you throw this book down in disgust, I am not saying that you can't have nice things. I have everything I ever wanted. My point is that Americans have been trained since birth to put the cart before the horse, to get the thing and then pay for it. This has had the collective effect of keeping us—even those who make a decent living—enslaved to the system.

Of all your friends and acquaintances, how many are truly free? If you know even one person who is, then you also know that the initial pain of living within your means is worth it. The borrower is slave to the lender. Always remember that. It will make you view debt as the anchor it truly is. You might think that you have enough to cover all of your debts and you're not strapped, so why listen to Scott and sell off this stuff? The answer is simple: I am trying to move you to step two, in which you create funds that exceed your needs, and the less debt you have, the faster and easier that journey will be.

What about the "good debt" everyone talks about? I am embarrassed to say that I bought into the good-debt hype for years. For those who haven't heard this pitch, the financial gurus call any debt that gets you a return on your money "good debt." For instance, if you borrow $50,000 against your home and use that money to purchase a rental house, and the rental income is higher than the payment on your $50,000 loan, some experts call that fifty grand "good debt." But is it really? If I had never experienced the crippling effect of the 2007 real estate downturn I might think so, but I learned the hard way that there is no such thing as good debt.

Debt is debt, and it's *all* bad—unless you're the lender. The goal is to be debt-free. Why do so many books and courses teach the opposite? Because everyone wants the quickest, easiest path to success, and success through debt looks easy. It can be accomplished tomorrow! What a nice blurb for a book cover—only, those authors don't tell you how easy it is to go bankrupt the day after tomorrow. It's very easy. Trust me, I've been there. *All* debt is bad, even the debt on rental properties, like the one I mentioned in the previous example. Even if a property is cash-flow positive by a few hundred dollars a month, the second that tenant stops paying or files a frivolous claim to delay an eviction or calls to report a leaky roof, your so-called good debt goes bad in a flash. The ideal way to buy rentals is slowly, free and clear. Don't be disheartened by this approach. If you follow step one and live within your means, you'll see that you don't need as many rentals as you think to realize your vision. There are ways to buy rentals without saving up for them, and we'll cover those strategies in chapter 9.

I asked you to create your vision before I presented these steps because focusing on your vision makes decision making easy. Whenever you're faced with a decision that involves reducing your debt or needs as part of step one, ask yourself, "Will doing this bring me closer to my vision?" If the answer is yes, do it. No more thought is required. Remember, sacrificing is not permanent. You only need to tighten your belt for a while as you begin doing things in the right order: money first, things second.

I wish I'd learned this approach when I was living on $2,000 to $3,000 a month. I would have eliminated massive risk and stress. I never would have fallen back to square one and had to start over. This is why I am sharing my philosophy. My greatest joy comes from liberating people who otherwise might have lived the rest of their lives enslaved.

Step Two: Create Funds That Exceed the Needs You Reduced in Step One

The rest of the book is focused on this step, which is where real estate comes into play. You can choose many vehicles for this step, and as I detailed in chapter 1, I've tested more than a few throughout my long career, from bars and sandwich shops to tanning salons and limo rentals. After trying a wide variety of businesses, I've made real estate my vehicle of choice. It's obviously one that interests you, too, or you wouldn't be reading these pages. It's a smart decision, in my opinion, because real estate done properly offers a high return, low risk, and endless variety. What does "properly" mean? Well, I've already shared some of my views on debt, which shapes the way all my systems work. In the coming chapters, I'll present strategies for a wide range of real estate investments. These will include:

- **Bird-dogging.** In this strategy, which has the lowest risk and the lowest profit, you locate properties that might be deals and refer them to investors for a fee.

- **Rehabbing.** You close on the property, renovate it, and then market it at a retail price.

- **Wholesaling.** You contract a property, mark it up, and then sell it to another investor who will rehab and retail it himself or herself.

- **Rentals.** You close on a property and put it in your long-term portfolio for residual rental income.

As part of step two, I will not only walk you through these and other strategies to push your income well above your expenses, I'll also teach you the fundamentals of deal making in a way that other books and seminars don't. I'll show you how to find buyers and sellers and tell you exactly what to say to each of them every step of the way.

Step Three: Create Real Long-Term Wealth

This is where your kids and grandkids get taken care of—not to mention those Lamborghini fantasies. In step three, you'll reinvest the excess funds you've created through multiple revenue streams. This is only possible if you have truly followed step one—eliminated debt and simplified your living expenses. You'll hit step three after you've been paying cash for everything and have significantly more money coming in each month than you have going out.

Step three is a joy to work through. Now you can give that money away, and it won't affect a thing. If a loan goes bad, it won't be a hardship. You can lend out your excess funds and multiply them or continue to purchase more free-and-clear rentals and build a real empire. The point is, you're free, and everything you do is your choice. You've built a snowball that can't be stopped, and you're choosing which hills to roll it down.

Our purpose here is learning how to make money through real estate, and that's what I'll devote the rest of the book to. I hope that by now you understand why I felt an obligation to first discuss the real goal—freedom—and coax you into forming a clear vision of how you would spend your days once you had it. I'm about to show you how to make a lot of money—remember the $100,000 guarantee that kicked off this book. But what's the point of making large amounts of money if you believe the end goal is more money? Such a view puts you right back on the hamster wheel, earning more but spending more again. You need to be prepared for the money you will earn when you follow my systems. You need to always remember that the goal is freedom, not money, and you need to follow the three steps we explored in this chapter. You can't skip the pain of step one—living within your means—and get to step two. It won't happen.

I have made and lost millions. I have had financial security while mowing lawns for a living and barely scraped by while running multiple businesses and a real estate portfolio worth many millions. I came by these principles the hard way, and I wish someone had given me this sort of guidance twenty years ago.

Now, let's talk real estate!

CHAPTER 3

THIS IS YOUR BRAIN ON REAL ESTATE

When I titled this book, I didn't mean to imply that you won't have to work on your journey to true wealth. The opposite is true. As I mentioned earlier, I named it *Work Just Gets in the Way of Making Money* because of the countless people who watched me build wealth over the years and approached me to learn how they could do the same thing. I've taken a lot of time to work with such people, and the most common complaint I get when I explain my systems is that, while the strategies sound great, no one with a full-time job can use them. It's easy for me, people say, because I have the time—but they're just too busy. Work gets in the way of their making money over and above their hourly wages.

I want to dedicate the first chapter of this book—where I detailed the many businesses I started, learned, managed, bought, and sold *while* I was learning how to invest in real estate—to those skeptics. No one knows better than I do just how hard it is to work a full day and then shift gears and work some more. The bottom line is, if you want it, you'll find a way. You can make excuses or you can make money, but you can't make both. Think how much time many of us could create just by skipping that *Seinfeld* rerun—the one you've already seen four times—each night. Do you want to watch *The Apprentice* or be the apprentice? You don't need forty hours a week to begin investing. A few hours stolen here and there will do it. Working on the weekends will do it. A simple routine change, such as getting up a little earlier each day, will do it. An excuse is the easiest thing in the world to find, but if you're determined, finding enough time to invest is pretty easy, too. The old adage has it right: if something is important, you find a way; if it's not, you find an excuse.

I said this earlier, and I'll say it again: not only do those of you with jobs not have to quit but you should not quit. Let me repeat: *do not quit your job!* You need to make a living until you get off the ground, and when it comes to mortgages, there are lots of advantages to having a job. It's not what you do at your job that makes you wealthy, it's what you do in your time off. If you're imagining that you would turn into a slave, working on real estate deals after you punch out or quit for the day, ask yourself, what are you now? Do you control your days? Do you control your income? Do you love the way you're spending those forty or fifty hours a week at the plant or in the office? The system you've been spoon-fed since you were a kid and forced into as an adult is the true slavery. I'm pointing you toward freedom. You need to see your investing efforts in these terms because your mind-set going forward is as important as any of the strategies I'll teach you.

Some of you might see the word "mind-set" and think this chapter's not for you. I'm already a positive person, you're thinking, but this is not just about being positive. The fact is, there are plenty of broke positive people. Everyone wants to be rich. Everyone wants a nice house and nice cars. Everyone can also read the same books and go to the same seminars, but not everyone will be successful. This is the land of equal opportunity, not equal results. Being positive is not enough—not even close. I enjoyed the movie *The Secret,* but it put too much emphasis on the power of positivity. Being positive is great, but where was the part calling on you to take action? According to *The Secret,* if your pool is green with algae, you simply believe it will be clear and, *voila,* it will happen. I'm here to tell you that you can stand poolside and repeat to yourself "the water is clear, the water is clear, the water is clear" until *you* turn green—but without a brush and a bucket of chlorine, that pool is staying as green as the Hulk.

The mind-set I'm talking about does encourage you to be positive, but my steps for getting there are practical. As with every part of this book, I'm going to give you the nitty-gritty, day-to-day steps you must take to get your brain on real estate. Right now, you're probably thinking like someone's employee. Take the simple steps I'm giving you—none of which requires much time—and within a couple of weeks I'll have you thinking like an investor. Here are the steps to follow.

DROP YOUR LOSER FRIENDS

Harsh? Yes. Necessary? Absolutely. You have to do this for many reasons. Here's a simple one: your loser friends get up in the morning and work all day for peanuts. The more money that you make and the easier you make it, the more they will resent you. Some members of your family will, too, but you're stuck with them. When you're feeling energized and enthusiastic about a new idea, your loser friends will be all too happy to tell you why it can't work, laughing about how much time you're wasting. Every one of them will relate the saga of his cousin or neighbor or friend, the one who tried real estate and lost his or her shirt.

Investing takes guts and hard work. It is much easier to shut off your brain and go to work every day and do what the boss says and think what your neighbors think and then retire. Henry Ford said it best: "Thinking is the hardest work there is, which is the probable reason why so few engage in it." The fact that you're reading this book and thinking about investing has already set you apart, and that distance from your friends is only going to grow. Do you need to officially break up with them? No, probably not. You can still be friends on paper, and the truth is, they'll soon begin keeping you at arm's length anyway.

You might have heard the old saw that you can tell how much a man makes by averaging the income of the five people he spends most of his time with. In my experience, this is absolutely true. We are attracted to like-minded people, aren't we? By taking positive steps to change your life and earn more, you're already thinking differently from your friends. The mere fact that you picked this book demonstrates difference, and the differences will become glaring as you start to make money and control your days. The odds are very good that your loser friends—and you might have some who aren't losers—won't want to learn how to do what you're doing. If anything, they'll want you to do it for them, and when you don't, their resentment will build. If there are some friends you can't bear to dump—as I said, many will dump you first, so you won't have to sweat it—your only other option is to lead. You will have to teach them to be motivated and, in essence, become their coach. Only the ones who have the desire to get motivated will follow you—a small minority, as you'll quickly learn. Not everyone wants a better life. Instead of wasting time on those who don't, you need to move on with yours.

Your spouse is another story. It's critical that you get him or her on board. I have seen many cases of people trying to invest while their spouses fought them the whole way, just waiting for a bump when they could say, "Told you so." In my opinion, it is so important to get your spouse on board that I recommend you wait until you have that support before moving forward. This is a tough business, with many ups and downs, and without your partner's support, something is going to fail—either the business or the relationship. Take your time, do what you have to, but get your spouse behind the effort.

Once you have your spouse's support and you've dumped your loser friends, you'll need to retrain your brain not just to be positive but also to see opportunities and possibilities. Without action, nothing happens, no matter how positive you are. The following steps offer practical ways to sniff out opportunities and see the possibilities invisible to most.

LEARN YOUR MARKET

You have to get to know your market because when you see a deal, you must be able to recognize it immediately and act quickly. I'll show you safe ways to do this. You want to be a person of action, not be reckless. The key difference between those two options is knowledge of the local market. This is what gives you the ability to make calls on the fly. The ability to act fast, by the way, is important even before you're ready to do deals. We make money in real estate, first and foremost, by *finding* deals. I cannot count the number of times I have come across a deal that for one reason or another I had no intention of purchasing. I was still thrilled. Once I know it's a deal, I immediately lock it up with an option and start marketing it to my investor list. This is the "easy money" that I'll discuss in a coming chapter (and don't worry about technical terms you might not know here—we'll cover them all later).

To recognize a deal, you should be constantly checking out the market and seeing where prices stand. To this day, I read every transaction in my area for the week in Saturday's real estate paper. I do this for several reasons, but the first is that I want to see what the deals sold for. I check on how much the deals that I didn't get went for, and I see what the ones I wholesaled (a strategy we'll discuss later) ended up selling for. I see who is doing a lot of transactions and what they're paying, and this gives me insight into what I might sell my deals for and to whom.

JOIN A LOCAL REAL ESTATE INVESTORS GROUP

Putting space between yourself and your loser friends is key, as we've discussed, but so is acquiring new friends. You can start by joining your local real estate investors group. Every area has one and some have several. These groups are great for meeting new people as well as for making an occasional deal, getting a property bought or sold. You'll pick up ideas and techniques from those with more experience, learn about legislative changes affecting real estate, and have the inside track on what's happening in the local market. At least this is what will happen if you join a good, active group. Be careful that you don't end up hanging out with a bunch of people who have never done a deal. You want to meet the players in your area, the people who do real estate full time. They generally won't mind talking to you and will be a great source for selling deals. Be sure to get everyone's business card.

DO LUNCH

Go to lunch with people in the industry. If you work a regular day job, it might be early coffee or a beer after work instead, but this type of social/business meeting is very important. I have been doing lunches for about ten years, and they have become one of my greatest sources of ideas and inspiration. To start, invite someone you met at the investors group meeting. Pick out some people who seem interesting and friendly or who do something you're interested in or something you would like to learn more about. Simply ask if you could buy them lunch one day and exchange ideas. You can also say that you want to find out exactly what kinds of deals they like in case you're able to send some their way. Offer to pay. I always do, and believe me, even well-off people rarely turn down a free lunch. Over the years, I've developed a standing lunch every Thursday with the same core group. This has been extremely useful for bouncing ideas off each other, solving problems, and exchanging deals. We call the group the "No-Work Club," though in reality we probably work more than most. If you are uncomfortable with calling a stranger and having lunch, another great option is Meetup.com. This website asks you to type in your interests and then sets you up with local groups of people who have similar interests. Many of them will have regular meetings or lunches you can attend.

CUT OUT THE NEWS

It's impossible to completely cut out the news, but unless it's related to local real estate, I suggest you do your absolute best to block it. This might sound crazy, but give it a try. What do you have to lose? Think of it as an experiment for the next month. Turn off talk radio, NPR, and the all-news stations. Skip CNN, Fox News, the BBC, and

MSNBC. Go right to the real estate section of your local papers and toss the rest. You do not realize how depressing it is every night to see that lady who killed her two-year-old, the latest health scare, or the toll of this week's mass shooting. All of that negative, distracting dreck is sapping your mental energy. Get rid of it.

Avoiding the news doesn't mean you'll become ignorant. I pick up enough browsing my Web homepage and talking to friends to know what's going on in the world, and if something sounds really interesting, I can look it up. Driving around to browse houses will give you excellent thinking time. Don't ruin it with the radio. This is the ideal time to turn on some real estate podcasts. That might sound boring, but you'll get used to them and even start to enjoy listening. Once you've listened to enough of them, doing so will become second nature, and you'll absorb things without even knowing it. Later, you'll wonder how you knew what a particular term meant or where you got the idea to do something. This is the beauty of a brain on real estate, sucking in useful information and eliminating static.

READ

Retraining your brain takes time. Happily eliminating news will free up both time and mental space that you can devote to reading. I'm not talking about *Harry Potter* or the *Star Wars* novels. There are many terrific books out there on business and real estate. Get them— your new acquaintances at the investors group and your lunches can recommend the latest—and immerse yourself in them. Try to read every day, even if on some days that means just ten minutes at night before you doze off and dream real estate dreams. I have read a vast number of books about real estate, and I've almost always taken away something useful from them. Some have revealed strategies I didn't know about or new techniques for finding and buying properties.

Even a mediocre book, however, might include one small tip that could make me an extra $50 a month per property. I also love to read books on the history of great companies. I'm a sucker for hearing the stories of how a Dell or a Starbucks got started. Seeing how ordinary people have created extraordinary enterprises is instructive and inspiring. Reading these books will put you in a results-oriented place.

SET CLEAR GOALS

You must set clearly defined financial goals. Yes, you've heard this a hundred times. You've heard it over and over for a reason—it's absolutely vital. You can't meet goals if you haven't delineated them in concrete terms. I'm not talking here about a three-item wish list, your hopes for vacations, or the kind of person you want to be. This is completely different from the aforementioned vision of how you'd like your life to look. What do you expect to accomplish financially in the next week? How about in a month, a year, five years, a decade? Be as specific as you can, and write these financial goals down. If they're not on paper, they don't count.

Don't be intimidated by this task. Most people don't realize that their goals are much easier to attain than they think. Writing them down makes them real, and accomplishing them one week at a time builds confidence. I like to set my goals by working backward, "reverse-engineering" them. First, I figure out what I ultimately want, the end goal, and then work backward to determine what it will take to get there. I begin by deciding on the material items or the dollar amount I'm aiming for and then break that down into a monthly cost over the coming years. My life primarily revolves around rentals, so I then convert that monthly cost into my currency: How many rentals do I need in order to achieve the goal I've set? I then can start thinking about my strategies for acquiring the rentals I'll need, collecting rents, and building equity year by year and month by month.

Here's an example. Let's say I determine I need $20,000 a month to retire in comfort. Many people would say that to meet that goal, you must save around $5 million and have it earn 5 percent interest. How long would it take you to save $5 million? Probably a lifetime, if not several. Today's CD rates are only around 1.25 percent, so finding a safe way to earn that steady interest would also be a challenge. But working backward, you can achieve the same result with twenty to fifty houses. If you pay cash or put them on short-term amortizations and accelerate the payoffs, you can accomplish the same result in ten years or less.

Have you ever purchased a new car and then noticed that same make and model everywhere? How is it possible that suddenly every third person drives your car? The truth is, those cars were always there—you simply never noticed them. Financial goals work the same way, and that's the real purpose of this step. Once you put a goal on paper, you'll start to see opportunities that can bring you closer to making it a reality all over the place. The opportunities were always there. You just weren't paying attention. Writing down goals makes you pay attention.

DECIDE YOU'RE READY

Lastly, you simply have to decide. You must decide that you have had enough and will not quit until you reach your goals. A little story about my friend and colleague Kevin will illustrate the point. I met Kevin's mother at the gym where I worked out three times a week. He'd recently graduated college and was interested in investing, and she wanted to know if I would have lunch with him to talk real estate. (Remember our tip about lunch? Kevin was already doing something right.) For the record, I wanted to have lunch with this college grad I'd never met about as badly as I wanted a root canal, but I felt obliged since I knew I'd be seeing his mother three times a week. Reluctantly, I agreed.

A few days later, Kevin and I had a good lunch, talked real estate for a few hours, and then parted ways. I'd done my part and thought that was the end of it. Kevin had other ideas. A few days later, he called and asked if he could work for me—for free. He would do whatever needed doing, no task too menial, and would take no pay in return. He just wanted to be around real estate investing. You could say that Kevin wanted his brain on real estate and saw me as a convenient way to get it there.

A free, highly motivated employee? How could I say no? Where was the downside? Every morning when I showed up to work, there sat Kevin in my parking lot. He would walk up to the office with me and hang around, doing whatever needed to be done, running to the bank to make deposits, driving out to a house to change doorknobs, delivering contracts, you name it. He never complained, and he never missed a day. We started calling him "the apprentice." It was pretty weird at first, I have to admit, having this guy tagging along everywhere, but it actually made me more productive. I couldn't just sit around with someone watching, could I? I had to be at the top of my game.

Over the years we became good friends and are now partners in about forty rental properties, a real estate business that flips fifty to sixty houses a year, and one of the fastest-growing property management companies in our area. Yes, Kevin learned his stuff. He has done very well for himself, and in the process, he helped me grow. It's a true win-win. What's my point? With no knowledge and less experience, Kevin made up his mind that he was going to be a successful real estate investor and kept at it until he succeeded. He decided that he'd had enough and was not going to quit until he reached his goals. If I'd turned him down when he offered to work for me, I guarantee that he would have found a berth with someone else. His approach was a little unorthodox, but Kevin knew instinctively that the fastest way to succeed was to begin thinking like an investor and that the best way to accomplish that goal was to get his brain on real estate.

ACTION PLAN

- Fire your loser friends (or at least demote them to part time).

- Start reading the local real estate section, including every sales transaction.

- Cut out the news.

- Join your local real estate investors group.

- Take at least three investors out to lunch to exchange ideas.

- Start reading real estate books, including one this week.

- Set clearly defined financial goals. They can and will change over time, but don't put this off—it's a vital part of getting started.

 C H A P T E R 4

INVESTMENT STRATEGIES: AN OVERVIEW

In this chapter, I'll present an overview of four key real estate strategies. If certain tactics, terms, or procedures seem confusing, don't worry—I'll go over my systems in greater detail later. The point here is to give you a broad overview so that the steps make sense as I explain them. For example, finding motivated sellers will be your first concrete step as an investor—and the biggest key to your success—but discussing that effort won't make much sense unless you first have some sense of the big picture.

I have designed my systems around single-family houses. I won't discuss commercial properties or apartments in this book. There is money to be made in those areas, to be sure, but they are complex arenas dominated by professionals. They're hard to understand and harder to break into, and they generally require access to banks and capital. Single-family investing, as I do it, requires only some basic knowledge and hard work. It's the easiest type of real estate investing to comprehend, the easiest to finance, and the most readily accessible. Everybody needs a place to live, and when it comes to single-family houses, we're talking about a person dealing with a person—

no banks or brokers, no big down payments or arcane rules written by and for lawyers.

The four main strategies we'll explore here are the ones briefly mentioned in chapter 2: bird-dogging, rehabbing, wholesaling, and rentals. First, I'll touch on bird-dogging and rehabbing. I don't recommend that you focus on either of these, especially starting out, but they are important parts of the business, and there might be times when you'll want to pursue one of these strategies. Mostly, you'll deal with others involved in bird-dogging and rehabbing, so it's important that you understand them. I'll then spend most of this chapter giving an overview of wholesaling—the type of investing I recommend you focus on—before concluding with rentals, which are an important part of creating long-term wealth, after you've gotten the hang of wholesaling and have started cashing checks.

The key to each of these strategies is finding deals—locating sellers who are highly motivated. This is *the* way that we make money in real estate. I will only touch on this pursuit here, since I'll spend all of chapter 5 exploring how to find motivated sellers. I want to emphasize, however, that it's the foundation of all four approaches and the most critical piece of the puzzle.

BIRD-DOGGING

The bird dog, as the name implies, tracks down properties that might be deals and refers them to investors for a fee. That fee varies but is often in the neighborhood of $1,000 to $2,000. It entails the lowest risk of our four strategies—and the least profit.

People often confuse bird dogs with wholesalers because the two are similar. The prime difference is that a bird dog never contracts a property and might not even contact its owner. Oftentimes, a bird dog simply locates a property that looks like a deal, gets the owner's contact info, and passes this along to an experienced investor. The investor will then contract the property if it's suitable in order to wholesale it (more on this shortly) or to rehab and sell it at a profit. Investors who use bird dogs pay them just a small fraction of what the investors will later make in profit—a kind of finder's fee. The bird dog might be active, scouring communities for potential deals, or passive, collecting info from homeowners responding to the bird dog's ads or signs.

What do we mean by finding "deals"? As I mentioned, we'll explore this cornerstone of investing in detail in the next chapter, but essentially bird dogs—like those pursuing any of our strategies—are looking for highly motivated sellers. Motivated sellers don't just *want* to sell, they *need* to sell. Real estate investors frequently mention the five or six "Ds" when discussing motivated sellers. The "D" words can vary but usually include some combination of: death, divorce, disease, debt, despair, and drugs. Couples in the midst of messy divorces or financial troubles might need to sell their homes quickly at discounted prices. The families of people who died and left homes behind them often want to dispose of such properties painlessly and don't mind selling below the market value to avoid hassle, and so on. The six Ds stand for the most common forces that create motivated sellers. Good bird dogs might find such properties because they have direct knowledge of homeowners' illnesses, changing marital status, or finances, but they also know how to interpret telltale signs of trouble—sudden neglect of lawns, trash or mail piling up, or utilities being turned off. Bird dogs sniff out the sellers who need cash now, and investors are willing to pay for this info.

Bird-dogging is tough, and I don't recommend it, for this reason: if you've done the difficult work of locating a deal, why not bring it full circle and go for the big check by wholesaling or rehabbing the property yourself? Why earn $1,000 for the hardest part of the process when you could earn $20,000? I love bird dogs in my business because they find me deals all the time, and I pay them relatively small fees for an invaluable service. But bird-dogging just doesn't make sense for anyone who wants to make serious money in real estate. I recommend that you use bird dogs as you see fit; let them help you develop your business, but don't become one.

Why would anyone bird dog? It makes sense for some people, especially those who don't want to pursue real estate investing but who have access to or inside knowledge of deals. For example, I have a financial planner who tips me off to likely deals on a regular basis. He has no interest in becoming a real estate investor, but he knows that I buy houses, so when he encounters someone looking to dump a property in the course of his work, he calls me. If I close on the deal, I bring him a check for $1,000. Everybody wins. I have a similar arrangement with a mailman, who, as you can imagine, often spots signs of change or distress in the houses on his route before for-sale signs appear. Others become bird dogs because they are simply so risk-averse that they're afraid to sign contracts under any circumstances. My sincere hope is that by the time you've finished this book, you will have the confidence to skip finding deals for a thousand bucks and instead go straight to doing the deals yourself for $20,000, $30,000, or more.

REHABBING

In rehabbing, an investor typically closes on a property, improves or "rehabilitates" it, then sells it at a higher price to turn a profit. Sometimes called "flipping" houses, rehabbing might be the best known of the four strategies we'll explore here, thanks to various television shows. The practice grew especially popular in the early 2000s before the real estate bust, when a booming market encouraged many would-be investors to get in the game. Rehabbers purchase homes that range from seriously distressed, with major structural or systemic problems, to properties that are merely neglected or a little outdated. The "rehab" can range from affordable, cosmetic improvements, such as fresh paint and new carpeting, to larger, pricier upgrades, such as new plumbing, roofs, and kitchens.

Minor, surface-level rehabbing is sometimes called "prehabbing" or "wholetailing." As I'll explain in the next section, wholesaling involves "flipping" the contract, not the house. With this strategy, we put the house under contract and then "assign" the contract to an investor for a fee, acting as the middleman. Sometimes, however, it pays to close on the house and improve it in some minor way that can significantly boost our profit. If you buy a hoarder house, for instance, and it's packed with stuff, you might only make $10,000 wholesaling it. Get a few dumpsters and a bunch of guys over to clean it out, however, and you can make $30,000. In this case, it's worth paying the closing costs and spending a week cleaning it up, so that you can sell the house to an investor at a price closer to its "retail" value—the market price an end user eventually will pay. This method is called "wholetailing" because it's somewhere in between wholesaling, where you're strictly a middleman, and rehabbing, in which you significantly improve the house and sell it at a retail price to the end user. Others call the process "prehabbing" because they do a minor rehab (a prehab) before an investor buys it to do a major one. If this seems confusing, don't worry—we'll come back to the concept later in greater depth.

I used to rehab all the time. For a while, it was my prime operation, and I enjoyed it. The upside is that it can be quite profitable. As middlemen, wholesalers necessarily leave some profit on the table for the investors they assign contracts to. They must, or the deals wouldn't make sense for their buyers. If a wholesaler makes $25,000 on a house, the investor who buys it to rehab might make another $25,000. Finding the deal, closing on the house, and then seeing the rehab process through to completion yourself in such a case would mean making $50,000 instead of $25,000.

Why pass up that profit? Well, for starters, rehabbing requires money—either your own or, more likely, a lender's. Some rehabbers use banks, though this can be challenging if you don't have sterling credit, established banking relationships, and significant assets. Instead, rehabbers typically use "hard-money lenders" to fund the purchase and the renovation of a property. Hard-money lenders only care about the value of the house, not your track record or credit. If a deal goes sour, they take the house and cover their loan. You might find this source of private money by joining real estate investment groups, perusing tax records, or simply by googling "hard-money lender" for companies that offer this service in your area.

I'll discuss "private money" in more detail later, but the point here is that rehabbing requires borrowing, which *always* entails risk—even when the loan is quickly repaid. Ideally, a rehabber should have a house renovated and on the market within four to six weeks of closing on it, but what if some unforeseen problem arises and he or she has to carry the property for months? Interest accrues, and profit is slowly siphoned off to the lender. What if the market tanks? What if an unforeseen structural problem appears? What if the rehab estimates were off? Wholesalers realize their profits the day they assign contracts for houses—and they never have to carry properties. The turnaround from signing a contract to assigning it to an investor-buyer can be as quick as a few days. Rehabbers, on the other hand, don't see their profit until much later, after the renovation has been completed and the home has been marketed and sold. Many, many things can go wrong during that period, and in my opinion, avoiding the risk and debt of rehabbing justifies leaving some profit on the table for an investor.

I got out of rehabbing because of the biggest inherent risk: contractors. If you don't babysit them, you get ripped off. It's that simple. Even good contractors will rip you off if someone doesn't monitor them constantly. I started traveling while I was rehabbing houses, which made keeping tabs on every step of the renovations difficult. In fact, I got ripped off twice in 2013, and then I asked myself, "Why am I still doing this? I value my time and my freedom more than a higher profit margin." That was when I decided to go back to wholesaling full time.

Perhaps you're handy and have considered rehabbing because you could do the renovation, or some portion of it, yourself. If rehabbing is a labor of love and you're excited by the idea of installing furnaces or hanging drywall, then perhaps DIY rehabbing will make sense for you as a kind of hobby, but I recommend against it, no matter how skilled you are. This book is for people who want to invest in real estate. If you decide to paint an investment house yourself, you're saving the cost of a painter, which in essence means you're earning the wage of a painter. Nothing against painters—painting is great, skilled work—but if that's what you want to do, don't be a rehabber, go be a painter. I am blessed in having no home improvement skills, so I've never considered fixing things myself. Those who are handy, though, inevitably are tempted to fix the air conditioning or install new windows themselves to save $800. But when you spend two weeks of your very limited time installing those windows, you stop being a real estate investor and become a window installer.

Here's a rule of thumb I will repeat throughout this book: spend your time on whatever puts you closest to the money. In other words, fill as much of your day as possible with the activities that have the highest payoff. Finding properties is your highest payoff activity—number one. Painting, mowing lawns, and laying carpet are among your lowest payoff activities. Outsource them—and all renovation and cleanup—if you decide to rehab a property. As I said, however, I recommend that you avoid the debt and risk of rehabbing in favor of wholesaling, which I'll discuss shortly. If you follow my advice, your only connection to rehabbing will be engaging in quick, cosmetic rehabs—prehabbing or wholetailing—on occasions when that strategy makes sense.

SPEND YOUR TIME ON WHATEVER PUTS YOU CLOSEST TO THE MONEY.

There are always exceptions, however. Some people truly love taking a dilapidated, ugly house and making it beautiful. If this sounds like a labor of love, as appealing as the whole idea of making money as an investor, then perhaps rehabbing is for you. Similarly, some investors enjoy dealing with properties but hate making deals. They don't want to talk to owners or negotiate prices. If this sounds like you, then you can rely on guys like me—wholesalers—to find and deliver the deals, so that you can focus on rehabbing. Even if you like the idea of rehabbing, however, I would recommend that you begin your investing career with wholesaling.

WHOLESALING

Why do I think wholesaling is your best bet as a new investor? Well, as I've mentioned, wholesaling requires no money—not from you or a lender—and no risk, but it produces substantial profits quickly. Here's how it works: the wholesaler finds a motivated seller, someone who will offer a "deal" on a house, and then signs a contract to purchase it. The contract is written up just as if the wholesaler intended to buy the house, but it has a provision that says that the contract is "assignable." The wholesaler schedules a closing date, as with any sale. Sometime before the closing, though, he "assigns" the contract to an investor-buyer. This buyer is now obligated to all the terms and conditions laid out in the initial contract, including the closing date. The assignment will be a one-page addition in which the wholesaler states that he contracted the property on a certain date with a particular party but is now assigning his rights and interest in this contract over to the new buyer for a certain amount of compensation.

If we think of rehabbing as flipping a house, wholesaling is flipping a contract. The wholesaler is a middleman who makes money from working out deals, finding motivated sellers, and matching their houses with investor-buyers. It's the buyer you assign the contract to who must find the cash. You don't have to borrow any money in the process, so you don't incur the risks associated with debt. In rehabbing, we buy low and sell high because the purchaser is typically an end user, a consumer paying a retail price for a house he or she wants to live in. In wholesaling, we buy very low and sell low because the purchaser is an investor who will improve the property and sell it for additional profit. The profit of the investor who will buy and rehab the house is built into the wholesaling process.

The new buyer pays you off when he or she signs and takes over the contract. The fees vary widely, but if you've done things correctly, they often range from $10,000 to $30,000, depending on the market. When I wholesale, I schedule my closings a maximum of thirty days out, meaning I always get paid within a month (and sometimes within a week). This is quite different from rehabbing, where the payoff might not come for three months, six months, or more.

The first concern of the novice investor is often "What if I can't find a buyer?" In the unlikely event that this happens, we include an escape clause in the contract. My contract (which I'll supply in chapter 7) has something called an "option to terminate," which lets you out of the deal if you can't find a buyer. This option exists solely for comfort. In more than twenty years of wholesaling, I have never had a deal that didn't close. If you follow my systems as I explain them in the coming chapters and buy actual deals according to the formula I'll supply, selling will be the easy part. Rehabbers are clamoring for houses like these every day of every week, and I'll teach you how to strike deals with them and build relationships.

Newcomers also often wonder if there's something devious about this process. Not at all. Assigning the contract doesn't affect the seller in any way. He or she gets absolutely everything agreed to in the contract, including 100 percent of the sales price. A different buyer will close—and make twenty grand on the deal—but that's not the seller's concern. Sellers simply want the price they were promised, and I make sure they get it, every time. The wholesaler essentially acts as a marketing company. We market for sellers, searching for deals, and then we market for buyers, trying to match those deals to the right investors. The wholesaler does not need a lender when acting as a middleman in this way. The only expense is whatever money you choose to spend on advertising, signs, business cards, etc.

Again, if this seems confusing, don't worry. Read on. This chapter offers a simple overview of wholesaling designed to give you a basic orientation. I have devoted a large part of this book to walking you through wholesaling techniques, with specific advice on how to find buyers, formulate offers, negotiate with sellers, etc. There are many good real estate books out there, but none have more specific, practical advice than the one you're reading now.

RENTALS

Like wholesaling, rentals are a vital part of my investment strategy. Remember the McDonald's Plan, my naïve strategy to become a millionaire by purchasing a million dollars' worth of houses—fifteen or so—and renting them out for thirty years at rates that covered the mortgages? I've already explained some of the flaws in this ill-considered approach, primarily revolving around maintenance and debt, but the connection between rentals and long-term wealth is a sound one. I am a wholesaler and I earn big checks wholesaling, but the minute I stop doing those deals, the checks stop, too. Rentals, on the other hand, are the gifts that keep on giving—even if you're too tired or sick to work or simply decide you'd rather spend a month or a year doing something else.

Later, I'll devote an entire chapter to my rental strategies and introduce you to something I call the "slow flip." Essentially, I buy low-end properties using private money and rent them out while paying off the debt as quickly as possible. Every market is different, but I typically buy my low-end rentals for about $30,000 per unit. I pay around 12 percent interest and amortize it over five years. Yes, like rehabbing, my rental strategy requires debt, which annoys me to no end. However, I'm out of that debt in five years, and then I own the rental free and clear forever. This is very different from the traditional approach, which makes you slave to a lender for thirty years.

What about the maintenance problems that drove me crazy in the heyday of the McDonald's Plan, a particularly painful issue when it comes to low-end rentals? I no longer deal with maintenance on my rentals, not ever. I said previously that I buy low-end houses and rent them out while paying off the mortgages in five years. In fact, I don't technically rent them. I sell them with long-term owner financing, using thirty-year mortgages. My tenant-buyers put $3,000 to $5,000 down and make monthly payments that cover my mortgage, taxes, and insurance (this math works on low-end rentals but not on higher-priced property). I'm a finance company to them, not a landlord, which means I'm no longer responsible for clogged toilets, repairs, or maintenance of any kind. They can't call me to plunge a toilet any more than they'd call Bank of America. This is the beauty of the slow flip—minimal debt and no maintenance—which I'll explain in detail later.

I recommend, however, that you hold off on purchasing rentals and building a long-term rental portfolio until you have gotten comfortable with wholesaling. Even more important, you should build up some cash reserves before you begin buying houses for your rental portfolio. My rule of thumb is to have at least three months of mortgage payments—whatever they will be—in reserve per property before I purchase rentals.

As I noted at the start of this chapter, finding the deals—locating motivated sellers—is the key to each of the four strategies I just laid out. It is how we make money in real estate, so we'll devote all of the next chapter to it.

ACTION PLAN

- Utilize "bird dogs" to help find you deals.

- Avoid the financial risks of rehabbing, aside from minor cosmetic updates.

- Consider wholesaling properties to obtain quick profits.

- Rent out your properties to achieve recurring income.

CHAPTER 5

FINDING MOTIVATED SELLERS

Before you can do a deal, you have to find a deal. This is how we make money in real estate, by "buying low," purchasing houses below their market value. In rehabbing, as I mentioned in the last chapter, we buy low and sell high because we're improving the property and selling it to an end user. In wholesaling, we buy very low and sell low because we're selling the property "as is" and leaving some profit for the investor who snaps it up to rehab. If we're building our rental portfolios, we buy low so that the monthly payments will cover our mortgage, taxes, and insurance until we own the house free and clear. The common denominator in all of these investment scenarios is buying low or finding a deal. This, as I highlighted in the last chapter, is *the* way to make money in real estate. Finding deals will be the most important part of your investment strategy.

How do you "buy low"? In order to spot a deal, of course, you need some sense of the market in your area. What are houses going for? If this sounds intimidating, don't worry. In the coming chapters, I'll show you the basics of how to assess a home's worth, analyze comparable properties or "comps," and formulate an offer. Meanwhile, as I advised in chapter 3, "This Is Your Brain on Real Estate," you should be scanning the recent sales in the local paper's real estate section and online. You should be driving through neighborhoods to see what's for sale, visiting open houses, and calling on for-sale signs even when you have no intention of buying. You will be amazed how quickly you'll develop a sense of what houses are worth in your area, which ones are overpriced, and which could have been priced higher.

Calling the numbers on signs and perusing ads gives you a great sense of the market, but these aren't necessarily the homes we're interested in. We're looking first and foremost for the houses that need to be sold yesterday, the sellers who'd like to skip the time-consuming hassle of brokers and marketing even if that means getting less for their houses. These are the "motivated sellers" I mentioned in the last chapter. We already covered the five or six "Ds" that real estate investors use to describe the forces that create motivated sellers: death, divorce, disease, debt, despair, and drugs. The sellers going through these crises will be your bread and butter because they want to dispose of houses quickly. If you feel uncomfortable reading that list, as if investors are a pack of jackals sniffing out carcasses to pick over, don't. Investors scouting for such deals provide a valuable service for people who have a dire need to dispose of property. A son or daughter who flew a thousand miles to deal with a parent's estate might not have the time or financial footing to wait months or even a year while a real estate agent markets the property. Getting quick cash for a house can help debt-ridden couples avoid bankruptcy, continue medical care, and end protracted divorce negotiations.

Massive numbers of people need to dispose of their houses quickly, for all sorts of reasons, and there are endless ways to find them. People who say there aren't any good deals out there just aren't working hard enough or smart enough. In this chapter, I'll show you some basic approaches for finding motivated sellers, mainly through various forms of advertising. I recommend that you try several of these techniques at once. If one isn't working, another will, and the method that was least productive this month might turn up the most leads next month. Start by casting a wide net, and I guarantee you'll begin finding deals.

VEHICLE LETTERING

Some of you, no doubt, have nice cars you'd rather not deface, but this basic form of advertising works. I was hesitant, too, back when I owned an Escalade, the first vehicle I put ads on. Reluctantly, I printed "WE BUY HOUSES" and a phone number on three sides of my precious SUV. "I can't believe you did that to an Escalade," my friends said, but the truth is, those ads paid for the car. The first year I had the vehicle lettered, it brought me several leads, and I closed one of them for a profit of $70,000. I decided that day that I'd never again have a car that wasn't lettered. Since then, I have probably made more than $250,000 as a result of leads that came from my vehicles. (Magnets are an option, of course, but when I see them, I think there's someone who just can't commit.) If you have a nice car, that's all the more reason to get it lettered. It will add to the impression that you are successful and have the means to buy houses. "When I saw those rims, I knew you were the guy who could help me," a seller who'd seen my car ad once told me. I made almost $25,000 on that deal.

BANDIT SIGNS

I don't particularly like bandit signs, but they work. These are the small, corrugated, plastic signs that you see on the side of the road. People call them bandit signs because, well, strictly speaking, they're not exactly legal in most areas. Advertisers must put them out at night or in the early morning to avoid problems. I know of just one person who actually got arrested for erecting bandit signs. Usually, the powers that be simply take them away or call with a warning. Apart from the legal issue, I resist bandit signs because so many people use them for so many businesses, they turn the street into a cluttered mess. I hated hanging these signs so much, I hired a guy to install and remove them for me.

If you decide to use bandit signs, my advice is to keep it simple: "WE BUY HOUSES" and your phone number. That works. When you try to explain your business or include a Web address, it's too much for passing drivers to read. I once made a batch of signs that said "STOP FORECLOSURE" and got a slew of phone calls from people who wanted to know how much I would pay them to stop my foreclosure. They thought I was losing my house and made signs to find someone who could stop my foreclosure. The "stop foreclosure" sign was a complicated flop. Stick to the simple stuff that works.

BILLBOARDS

Billboards produce great leads, and I use them, but they're expensive. I recommend staying away from billboards if you're starting out because the cost per lead is high. If you do use billboards, develop a brand first, something catchy. Choose specific colors and a logo that you can use in all your marketing materials. You want sellers who see the billboard to be able to contact you through other media and to recognize your brand elsewhere if they come across it.

TV COMMERCIALS

Like billboards, TV commercials produce great response but are quite pricey. They're worth the money, in my opinion, but only if your other systems are not generating enough leads. If you decide to go the TV route, spend the extra money and have your commercials professionally produced. We've all seen commercials that look like children shot them on cell phones. Such spots don't exactly inspire confidence. If I'm in a jam and trying to sell my house, I want a professional who is smarter than me to help—not some idiot with a talking dog that barks out, "We buy rouses!"

CLASSIFIED ADS

When I started in this business, one of my favorite sources of leads was a tiny classified ad in the local newspaper. I was one of many real estate investors, but the ads still produced great results for a comparatively low cost per lead. Today, however, newspapers are truly dead. To give you just one example, last June I received a phone call from someone trying to rent a particular house. He described the property, and I told him it was no longer available—and hadn't been for some time. The caller told me he'd just seen an ad for this home in the paper. Confused, I called the advertising department to see why the ad, which should have stopped in December, was still running. The ad manager apologized for the mistake and, of course, didn't charge me. I should hope not. That ad had been running for six months, and the first phone call it produced was the one alerting me to the mistake. Every community is different, however, and in some, newspapers still move real estate. If you live in one of these, you might test some classified ads, but track the results vigilantly to make sure you aren't wasting money.

BUSINESS CARDS

Business cards give the best bang for the buck, especially these days, when companies offer them so cheaply online. Once again, I suggest you keep it simple. Place "WE BUY HOUSES" in large bold print, and include your name and phone number. I also print "$500 referral fee for leads that we close" on the back. This can stir up business, and it encourages people to save your card.

REAL ESTATE AGENTS

We generally want to reach sellers before they hire real estate agents, but you would be surprised how many houses brokers list at ridiculous, below-market prices because the owners need quick sales. Some of these houses are inherited, and some belong to desperate sellers who bypassed the "we buy houses" people and went to an agent. Agents also list bank-owned foreclosed properties, which often sell for a song. Agents can be helpful, but remember that not all are created equal. You need to find one who can spot a deal and isn't afraid of low-ball offers. I've had agents solicit my business and then start emailing me about every house they encounter, deal or not. I don't have time for that flood of time wasters, which undercuts the whole point of paying an agent.

A good real estate agent will value the nature of your business and the recurring income it can produce. The average homeowner buys a house every five to seven years. We buy five to seven houses a month. Agents provide great collateral value, too. They often have useful information about various communities and niche housing markets, and they can help you find comparable properties if you're considering a house—even if you're not buying it from them. Always give the agents you work with your business when you're buying a listed property. Remember, they're in business too and trying to make a living.

DOOR KNOCKING

I should say straight away that many frown on this method and will brand its practitioners as "bottom-feeders." Door knocking didn't appeal to me either, but about ten years ago, one of my coaching students asked me to go on an appointment with him to help close a deal. I went with him, and he got the house, a great bargain. When I asked him how he'd found it, he told me that he used the direct-mail technique I'd taught him but hand-delivered the materials. The owner of the house happened to be home. They got to chatting and set up an appointment. After watching my student in action, I tried knocking on doors myself. I hated it and only did it a handful of times. I don't have the stomach for having people shoot daggers with their eyes or yell at me to beat it.

Some people, however—my student, for example—love knocking on doors, so I hired a guy to do it for me. He did a phenomenal job for a couple of years. I bought about sixty homes that I learned about from his knocking on doors. I paid him $1,000 for every house he contracted that made it to closing. He loved talking to the people he met, and they seemed to love him. The process worked out well for my guy because he had no investment and no risk. When he worked for me full time, he typically earned around $3,000 a month but had some months where he earned as much as $8,000.

If you want to try this method, here's how to go about it. Find the houses in the foreclosure section of the newspaper that meet your criteria and focus on the ones that seem to have enough equity to make sense. Equity, as you probably know, is the difference between the market value of the house and the amount the owners still owe. It's the amount of "money in the house," as we sometimes say, or the amount that can be taken out of it. If I owe $50,000 on my mortgage for a house worth $90,000, I have $40,000 of equity in the house. From the newspaper, you can get the dollar amount and date of the current mortgage. Next, look up the most recent assessment of the house on your local municipal website, where it will be part of the tax records. You can also find this info with other online tools, such as Zillow. These sites often contain inaccuracies, but for prospecting purposes they can give you a reasonably good idea of whether or not you should bother knocking on the door.

Now you need to do some calculating that factors in the way amortization, or loan repayment, works. If you've ever bought a house, you know that the bulk of your early mortgage payments are devoted to interest; the percentage of your payments devoted to the principal—the actual value of the house—is low. As a result, home-buyers tend to build very little equity in their homes during the first decade of making payments. After fifteen years, the average home-buyers might have about 20 percent of the home's value in equity. If the current owners have only been in the home five or six years, they will have paid almost nothing off the principal and will probably have very low equity. They are poor prospects. Equity can increase in other ways, however. If the owners paid for major improvements over the years—a spacious addition, say—or if the neighborhood improved dramatically—it's become a "hot" area—a house's value could have appreciated significantly, which would increase the sellers' equity.

My personal rule of thumb is that prospects should have at least 35 percent equity in a house for me to consider a deal. This means that if homeowners have a house valued at $100,000, I need them to have at least $35,000 in equity for the deal to work. In that scenario, I would pay up to 65 percent of the market value for the house, or $65,000 *minus* the cost of repairs. I have friends who pay more, but 65 percent of the market value (what the home will sell for after it's fixed up) is as far as I'll go. If the owners don't have 35 percent equity, they can't sell to me at a price that will make the deal work.

If this seems confusing, don't worry. I will explain it further in chapter 6, "Fielding Calls and Presenting Offers." For now, just remember that you want prospects with at least 35 percent equity in a house. Sometimes the calculation is easy. If you see from the paper that a seller's mortgage was for $100,000, and a recent assessment of the house values it at $200,000, you have a great prospect. If the mortgage on another house is for $150,000, the owners have been in the house ten years (not long enough to build much equity), and it's now valued at $170,000, it's highly unlikely you could make the deal work.

Once you've identified prospects from among the foreclosures, go knock on those doors. When someone answers, present yourself as a professional investor and offer to help him or her with the foreclosure problem. More often than not, they will slam the door in your face. Remember, most of these people are not just behind on their mortgages. By the time you meet them, they're probably behind on everything and ignoring a steady stream of calls from angry creditors and bill collectors. Now, here you come, a total stranger, to discuss the house they're about to lose. You might be the first investor to approach them about the house, or several others might already have come by, the owners' irritation growing with each one. Be as tactful and sympathetic as possible and leave immediately if it becomes clear you're not welcome. If the owners aren't home, leave your materials with contact info.

DIRECT MAIL

Direct mail is a little pricey and seems hit or miss, though I still use it. The key, I have found, is consistency. I recently closed a great deal that came from direct mail, and the seller told me that the letter I'd send out sat for a year in her files. This sort of scenario makes quantifying your results difficult. If you're going to use direct mail, don't try it one time and expect it to work. Don't take six or eight months off between mailings. Try a steady program of mailings over the course of a year, and do your best to track the results.

I do direct mail several ways. I send letters to the foreclosures that seem worthwhile, introducing myself and asking the owners if they'd like to discuss selling. This is inexpensive because it's so targeted. I include a copy of my usual letter here. I also will assemble

a list of houses that look distressed, properties whose owners might be motivated to sell, and mail them letters or postcards. This approach, too, is highly targeted and inexpensive, but it requires serious labor since someone has to scout those houses.

My final method involves mass mailings. It's far more expensive than the other two strategies, but it also generates more leads. You can refine your search by renting mailing lists of particular groups—out-of-state owners, owners who have been in their houses more than twenty years, people behind on their mortgages, etc. Filters like these can boost the percentage of good leads, but unfortunately you will still get many calls from people telling you to stop clogging their mailboxes. You can purchase these lists from companies such as ListSource.com and send mailers yourself, but most direct-mail companies also offer these lists and will handle mailings for you from start to finish. This is a better approach, I think, since your time is limited. Why take on an annoying administrative task someone else can probably do better? I use a number of companies for mailings, including Click2Mail.com, PostcardMania.com, and FastYellowLetters.com.

INTERNET

I am not especially computer savvy, but I realized long ago that the Internet is a powerful tool that can't be ignored. You *must* have a website, and while it doesn't have to be fancy, it should look good and work smoothly. When you meet with prospects, the first thing they'll do after the appointment is google your company name and check out your website. Your site is a reflection of your business and professionalism, so if it looks cheap and cheesy, that's what prospects will think of you. Building a nice looking, functional website doesn't cost much these days. Ask friends for advice on who can create one for you or browse online for Web developers.

I know of several investors who get their leads exclusively from the Internet and do quite well. Online advertising is efficient because you pay per "click," when consumers respond to your ad, not when they see it. Those clicks are measurable, which makes Internet marketing easy to monitor and tweak. When you market online, you obviously will direct people to your website. Some investors also direct prospects to their websites in offline marketing, but I don't. My opinion is that if I'm marketing offline, I always want sellers to call me. They already have my information in their hands, so why would I send them online, where all of my competitors also have ads? This is just my opinion, and others would disagree, but I separate the two. If I find a prospect offline, I try to keep them offline and get them on the phone. If they come to me online, I direct them to my website. The best source I have found for creating real estate investor websites is bestinvestorsites.com.

REFERRALS

This strategy, the least complicated and most familiar, is also by far the most effective source of leads. Referrals don't bring me the most leads, but they do bring me the best and easiest leads. These deals are the easiest to close because someone that sellers know and trust referred them to me. This person has already told the sellers that I'm a good and honest investor who can help them with their problem.

There are many ways to build your referrals, but the most effective is to pay referral fees. I generally pay $500 cash for a referral. I always pay it fast, and I never make the person referring me ask for his or her fee. No one wants to chase you down for money. I make sure to pay even when the person giving the referral doesn't know I've done a deal, as sometimes happens. Often, a deal doesn't happen until several months after the referral. In those cases, people are surprised and appreciative when you show up with unexpected cash. On your end, it's the right thing to do, and this business is filled with snakes and crooks, so when people find an honest investor, they keep the referrals coming.

I once had a young woman pull over to talk to me because she saw the "$500 referral fee" printed on my rear windshield. She referred me to her father, who brought me a deal I did very well on. The daughter earned her $500, which was all she cared about.

These are the basics of finding leads, but the previous list is by no means exhaustive. There are so many unorthodox ways to locate deals that I wrote a whole book on the subject, *The Real Estate Investors Guide to Guerilla Marketing.* That book is for the more advanced investor and includes techniques ranging from Facebook to Frisbees. The eleven lead sources listed previously, though, are more than enough to get you started. You can't afford to do all of them at once, especially not now, when you're getting started, but try several. If one isn't working, another will, and some will become more or less productive at various stages for no apparent reason. Time after time, I get calls from coaching students, complaining they aren't getting enough leads. I always respond with a list of marketing tasks. Are you putting out bandit signs? Are you calling on for-sale signs and ads? Are you attending investor group meetings? Have you tried direct mail? Usually, within a month of strict marketing coaching, leads are popping up and the problem fades away.

ACTION PLAN

- Read the recent sales in the real estate section, visit open houses, and call on for-sale signs to get a sense of the market.

- Get your vehicle lettered. (If you drive a junker, wait on this one.)

- Get business cards made. (Keep them simple, and check out Vistaprint.com.)

- Start talking to real estate agents to find one you want to work with.

- Get your website made. (Try bestinvestorsites.com.)

- Draft a letter you can use in targeted mailings or larger mass mailings.

- Run a simple classified ad: "WE BUY HOUSES" and a phone number.

- Hand out your card to anyone and everyone. (Most people either have a house for sale or rent or know others who do.)

CHAPTER 6

FIELDING CALLS AND PRESENTING OFFERS

Marketing is a vital part of real estate investing—in fact, as a wholesaler, you essentially are a marketing company—but for my money, the real fun starts after you've done your marketing, when the phone begins to ring. This is when the process gets real: *I'm actually getting calls and preparing to make offers!* If you're anything like me, this will be thrilling the first time it happens, but like that first leap off a diving board or run down a ski slope, it can also cause panic. Relax. We're going to make sure you've done all your homework and that you know exactly what to say and do to close the right deal and to walk away from the wrong one. In this chapter, I'll take you through the process of fielding calls, evaluating houses, and making appointments. With a practical hands-on approach that eliminates guesswork, I'll also show you exactly how to formulate and present an offer.

PEOPLE ARE CALLING! WHAT DO I DO?

You have put your number out there, passed out cards, switched on the website, and met some real estate agents, and now the phone is ringing. What do you say? How should you act? You don't want to seem like a complete novice, but you don't yet have any real experience either. In time, this will all get easier, but for now you'll just have to practice. The key is to sound confident and answer questions as best you can. If you don't know the answer to a question, just tell callers you will have to get back to them on that one. Do not make up answers, and don't lie. You can tell people that you have been involved with real estate for many years because this is true. You grew up in real estate and you work in it. You have bought or rented it for yourself over the years. You have always been around real estate. But don't tell callers that you have been buying and selling if you haven't. They will see right through you, and the trust will be gone. Without trust there can be no deal.

Some people will want you to tell them what you would be willing to pay for the house over the phone. I never do that. I can't. I don't have nearly enough information at that point to give an accurate offer. If callers ask how I come up with my offer, I tell them, "We do research in your neighborhood to see what houses like yours are selling for and how long they are taking to sell. Then we consider what kind of work the house would need to be in top-notch condition. We punch all of that information into the computer, and it calculates the offer. It would be impossible for me to determine all of this without doing a full evaluation."

I use a dedicated number in all of my marketing so that when that phone rings, I know it's a caller responding to an ad. I don't want my most important calls to be mixed up with tenant calls or personal calls. This is a good practice, but you don't need a separate phone when you're starting out. Save that expense for now and get a dedicated phone line later, after you've cashed a few checks.

When I get a call, my whole objective is to set an appointment. I do not negotiate or attempt to buy the house over the phone. Here's how a typical call goes. I answer, saying, "Thank you for calling (business name). This is Scott speaking. How can I help you?" The caller will say something like, "I saw your advertisement that said you buy houses, and I wanted to see if you would be interested in buying mine." I respond that I would definitely be interested and tell them that if they can give me some basic information, I'll see what I can do. Always get callers' names, addresses, phone numbers, and anything that they can tell you about their houses. Find out the number of bedrooms and bathrooms, the square footage, the age of the house, and any distinguishing features. Ask them what sort of condition it's in and what improvements, if any, they've made over the years.

You should also find out where callers heard about you and jot this down. This is key information. You must track which advertising is producing results so that later you'll know how to spend your marketing budget and can figure out the cost per lead of various methods. Get all of this information early in the call so you don't forget, and take notes on everything the caller says. You never know what information might prove useful later or what details you might forget or confuse between calls. Write *everything* down, and date each call in your notes.

I make it clear that I can't buy every house I see but that I would be happy to come by and make an offer. Tell callers that you are a professional investor who buys houses quickly, at a discount, in order to make a profit. Ask if that sounds like something that could work for your caller. When I started investing, I never explained this. I thought that if I could just get a foot in the door, I could later convince homeowners to sell at a discount. Eventually, I realized that

I was wasting my time and the sellers'. Most people who won't sell at a discount, can't, because they don't have enough equity in the property.

Do not set the appointment for a date too far off. Remember, these are motivated sellers. They have a problem, and if you can't solve it quickly, one of your competitors will. I have an investor friend who thinks he's the busiest person in the world. I've been with him when he gets a call from a prospect who wants to sell, and he sets the appointment a week or two out. I just shake my head. We are in a competitive business. I treat buy calls like fire drills. If a motivated seller calls, I try to schedule the appointment for a day or two later. If it's possible, I'll often head out to see the property the same day I get the call. This sort of quick response is good for you and good for the seller.

Starting out, you should go on as many appointments as you can, even if the owners don't have enough equity in the house to make a deal. Each appointment will be like a class for you, and you can learn as much from the ones that don't pan out as you can from the ones that become deals. "Practice appointments" boost your confidence, and after enough of them you will feel like a pro when a good deal does come along. It takes a while to get comfortable sitting in strangers' living rooms, getting to know them, and chatting about a major financial decision at a stressful time.

Last but not least, always be courteous and pleasant on the phone. This is your first step in building rapport with the seller, and you need to put your best foot forward to build trust. That's it. Congratulations! You just set an appointment.

DUE DILIGENCE

Now that you've set an appointment, it's time to get to work. Before you go on any appointment, it's important to complete your "due diligence," gathering background on the property. I start by checking to see if the house has ever been in the MLS, or multiple listing service. As you probably know, an MLS is a computerized system used by real estate agents to share information about properties and facilitate sales. If you do not have access to the local MLS, call the real estate agent you've chosen to work with. He or she can pull up the listing and send you info. The MLS provides good background— a picture of the house, the number of bedrooms and bathrooms, the square footage, etc. Photos are especially important because sometimes you review the sales of comparable properties only to visit the house you're considering and find that it's the one oddball in the neighborhood, nothing like the other properties you reviewed. These days, simply googling a house address often will lead you to photos and info about the property on sites like Trulia and Zillow. This, too, is good background, but as I've mentioned, these sites often contain inaccuracies, so don't take their word for anything, especially not the estimated value of the property. If the same house appears in photos on the MLS, as well as on Zillow and other sites, and all of them say it has three bedrooms, two baths, and 1,600 square feet, this will probably prove true. As you'll see, however, it's not unusual for one site to say a home has three bedrooms and for another to claim it has two. Assemble as much info as you can, and don't skip the MLS listing. It's more comprehensive than the others and less likely to contain mistakes.

Next, pull the tax records for the property. These are available online in most places these days, often at a county or state website. I don't give much credence to tax assessments, but I still like to get all of the information I can from these records: date and amount of last transaction (when the house sold), years owned, lot information, etc. After you have all of the specifics, check out your "comps," the prices that comparable properties nearby recently sold for, to get a sense of the property's market value. Many websites help you find comps, or you can once again solicit the help of your agent. I suggest that you do both in the beginning. If your Web searches are producing the same numbers as the agent, then you'll know that you can find the comps on your own. Zillow, Realtor.com, and other websites offer help with comparables, but my favorite is Realquest.com. This site costs money to use, but in my experience it offers the most and best information by far.

You should find at least three comps, but preferably more, especially early on. Try for six or seven at first. These should be regular retail sales, not short sales or sales of bank-owned properties. Comps help you establish the after-repair value (ARV) of the house. You need to know this number because you're going to try to get the place at a discount, for some amount significantly below what the market would bear if the home were fixed up, listed with a real estate agent, and marketed in a traditional manner. The idea, as you know if you've ever bought or sold a house of your own, is that the property would probably sell for around the same amount as similar or "comparable" properties in roughly the same location. Ideally, you want to look at houses as similar as possible, with the same type of construction, number of bedrooms and baths, and square footage. The closer their locations to the house you're considering, the better, and the more recent their sales dates, the better. If the market was booming a couple years ago but has sagged since, comparables that sold eighteen months ago might not reflect the reality of today's market. Conditions probably haven't changed in the last few months, however, so recent comps are a better bet. If you have six or seven comps, use the lower-priced ones when figuring your offer. Later, when you want to sell, you'll consider the higher-priced comps. This approach builds some cushion into the deal, boosting your security and profit.

Previously, I said you should focus on regular retail sales when looking for comparables, not short sales or sales of bank-owned properties. This is true—however, you should keep a separate list of all the similar bank-owned properties and distressed sales you can find. You will not need those for your ARV, but you will need them later when determining an offer.

Once you have an idea of what the property is worth, drive by the house and its comps. This is important because sometimes a computer can't tell the whole story. Your house might have a completely different design from the other comps you pulled. It might be on the wrong side of the tracks and have drug activity nearby. You can always fix a house, but you can't fix the neighborhood, so driving by is essential in determining your offer. The other day, I drove by a house that seemed perfect by the numbers. Everything I looked at online and in the MLS made it look like a great deal. When I did my drive-by, however, I noticed a cemetery on *both* sides of the house— an instant deal breaker.

APPOINTMENT ETIQUETTE

After you've checked out the comps, estimated the house's after-repair value, and done your drive-by, it's time to go on the appointment. Do not drive your "WE BUY HOUSES" vehicle to meet with the prospect. If you only have one car, trade yours with a friend's or spouse's for a few hours. This was another lesson I learned the hard way. When you pull up at someone's house in a vehicle all lettered up, the neighbors will take notice. After you leave, you can bet that a neighbor will walk over and say something like, "Hey Bill, I saw you had the We Buy Houses guy over. Are you selling your house?" When Bill says, "Yes, he's giving me $50,000 for it," the neighbor will offer $55,000. The next day, you're getting a call from your sellers telling you that they have changed their minds or asking if you can top $55,000. Either way, the lettering that was earning you money has now cost you a bundle.

You must have a firm grasp of the after-repair value (ARV) when you walk into your appointment. Just as the object of the phone call was to get an appointment, the object of the appointment is to leave with a contract. If you do not know your numbers ahead of time, you can't make an intelligent offer. Even if you have the numbers down, however, appointments can feel awkward at first. The homeowners have asked for your help with their housing problems even though you might not have enough cash or credit for a pack of gum. This appointment is the most important step in the whole process.

First, try to build rapport—a key step in most types of sales. Your sellers will decide very quickly if they like you, and if they don't, the deal might disintegrate even though it makes financial sense for all involved. People want to do business with people they like. In fact, they might actually accept a lower offer from you solely because you've established a connection and they trust you. The best way to build rapport is to ask questions and let them do the talking. People love to talk about themselves and seldom get the chance to. Bring up topics by listening to their answers and by looking around the house. For instance, if you see pictures of fish on the walls, you might ask them about fishing and then tell them of your fishing experiences. Ask about photos of their kids and volunteer something about yours, but let them fill most of the conversational space.

Don't just pretend to be interested. I'm not suggesting that—they would see right through it. Instead, choose points of intersection you're both genuinely interested in. Good rapport dramatically increases the number of deals you'll do. Done correctly, this step can last a long time without any mention of the house. Stay away from real estate talk until you've gotten comfortable and built rapport. Occasionally, though, sellers won't want to talk to you at all. They simply demand a number. If this is clearly the case, don't push them into conversation—just give them your offer.

Once you've built rapport and feel comfortable, ask the million-dollar question: why do you want to sell? This is important because often the problem necessitating a sale is not money. There are endless answers to this question, but whatever theirs is, pay close attention. If money is the issue, things probably will be cut-and-dry. If the answer involves divorce, death, a bad rental, illness, etc., the situation can be more nuanced, and a successful deal might be about more than a dollar amount. Some sellers might want to leave all of the unwanted possessions amassed in the house on the premises when they go. Sometimes they have an attachment to the home and want to be invited back to see it after the rehab. I had one buyer whose top priority was that the neighbors never learn her house was for sale until she moved out. The possibilities are limitless, but if you find out the real reasons people are selling, the buying process will be easier.

Ask the seller if they would mind showing you around the house. As you take the tour, you'll fill out a repair analysis worksheet (RAW). I've included one of these helpful tools in the appendix, and you also can print my blank RAW forms from this Web address: www.scottsresources.com. As you can see on the sample RAW form, just about every home repair imaginable is listed, with dollar amounts that make it easy to calculate each job. Painting costs about

$2.25 per square foot, so if the house needs painting, you multiply the square footage to be painted by $2.25 to calculate the cost of this improvement. Windows cost around $250, so if the place needs new windows, when you get to that line, multiply the number of windows needed by $250 (ten new windows cost $2,500), etc. My home improvement skills don't extend much beyond changing light-bulbs, so I rely heavily on this guide, which makes figuring repair costs a snap.

Talk while you walk. Ask what happened here, if you see damage or stains from water, for example. Find out how old the roof is. Ask if the plumbing and wiring are original or if they were replaced at some point. Did the current owners ever install a new furnace or hot water heater, and if so, when? Does the place ever flood? Does that fireplace work? Take your time and note everything, making notes and taking measurements. After you have done a couple hundred of these, you'll pretty much know your rehab numbers at a glance, but I recommend going through this step even if it's just for show. A thorough inspection will set you apart from the other investors who are just shooting numbers out. You will see some dilapidated, dirty houses in this business, but *never* make negative comments. The house might be the most disgusting you've ever seen, but if you insult its owners, the deal is dead.

After you finish your tour and complete a RAW, tell the sellers that you need to hop on your computer in your car and punch in the numbers, if that's okay with them. You'll be back in fifteen minutes with an offer. As you head for the car, casually throw out the big question, almost as an afterthought: "Do you mind if I ask you how much you're hoping to get for this house?" They won't always answer—many sellers want to hear your number first. It's important to ask, though, because sometimes sellers actually want *less* than you're willing to pay. If my offer was going to be $100,000 and the sellers tell me they were hoping for $80,000, guess what? My new max is $80,000. That question just saved me $20,000. There is nothing wrong with this. You're still solving their problem and giving them the price they want. It's a win-win. Sometimes the opposite happens, and they name a number that's way too high. In that case, I immediately tell them that I can't come even close to their price but that I'll figure an offer anyway so that they have a starting point. This might lead to a stalemate, but sometimes planting that seed alters their expectations. It's amazing how far a hoped-for price can fall during the fifteen minutes I spend in my car.

DETERMINE YOUR OFFER

With your filled-out repair analysis worksheet in hand and some sense of the sellers' situation, head to your car to compute the offer. This is a crucial part of the process and shouldn't be taken lightly. A mistake here can cost you dearly. If you're conscientious about following these three steps, however, figuring the offer will not be difficult.

Step One

As I described at the start of this chapter, you must spend time before your appointment determining the home's after-repair value, or ARV. This number represents how much the house would sell for on the retail market if it were in top-notch condition. Look at the number you've come up with based on several comparables with similar bedroom and bath counts, square footage, etc. Make sure the number still seems reasonable now that you've seen the house. If you've discovered, for instance, that there's a pool or a full finished basement you didn't know about, you might need to adjust this number up. If railroad tracks run through the backyard, you might have to adjust it down. Remember, though, the ARV is the price the home would fetch in mint condition. Don't alter this number because of the problems or distressed elements you just saw. We'll account for all that in a minute, using the repair analysis worksheet.

Step Two

Process the data on your RAW. As we saw in the last section, the RAW has lines for various items needing repair or replacement, everything from cracked plaster and flaking paint to leaking roofs and broken water heaters. Go through the RAW you filled out on the house tour, add up the dollar amounts on each line, and put the total at the bottom in the space provided. My biggest piece of advice in this step is don't underestimate repairs. Remember, this house has to be in top-notch condition in order to sell. Even if the carpet is only a year old, it will have to be replaced. Appliances, too, must be new for a retail sale—it doesn't matter that they work perfectly. I have tried rehabs both ways, and believe me, whatever money you save by cutting corners, you waste on carrying costs because the house will take longer to sell. I learned the hard way to figure in *all* the repairs and upgrades, and the RAW makes this easy.

Step Three

Take the house's after-repair value (ARV), which you examined in step one, and multiply it by 65 percent. This multiplier builds in profit for both you and the investor who will buy the property from you later. You must pay significantly less than the house will later fetch in a retail sale after it's fixed up, or the deal won't make sense for you and the rehabbers you'll pitch it to. Sixty-five percent of ARV is my own personal formula, as I mentioned in chapter 5, developed over years of trial and error. I have friends who go as high as 80 percent. I think they're crazy, but it seems to work for them. In my experience, 65 percent is a good safe number. Now, deduct from this new number the total for repairs and improvements that you calculated on your RAW, the number listed at the bottom of that form. Just as you built profit into the deal by multiplying the ARV by 65 percent (leaving at least 35 percent of the retail price for yourself and the rehabber who'll later buy it), you must build in the cost of repairs.

Here's an example. If you determined that the house's ARV is $100,000, you multiply this by 65 percent to get $65,000. Next, you subtract from this number the total for repairs on your RAW. Let's say the repairs and improvements totaled $20,000. Subtracting this from $65,000 gives us $45,000. This is your offer.

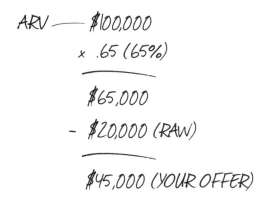

But before you write that number into the contract, you have one last thing to consider—those bank-owned properties and distressed sales you collected info on before you came out to meet the sellers. These are important because if the area has been hit hard by foreclosures, there might be active listings for less than your offer of $45,000. If that's the case, you'll have to adjust your offer down until it's below the other comparable distressed houses on the market. There is no reason you should pay more for this house than you would pay the banks for theirs.

That's it! You have figured out how much to offer. The process is fairly simple when you have the right tools and information. In a moment, you will fill out the contract with all of the information you have as well as your freshly calculated offer price. First, though, you should adjust the offer price by a couple of dollars to make it less square. For instance, if the offer was $45,000, I might change it to $45,178. I do this to give the impression that it is a scientific, to-the-dollar calculation I'm unlikely to sway from. This discourages sellers from trying to negotiate up. That little trick has made me tens of thousands of dollars in profit I would have lost had I left my numbers even.

Congratulations, you've determined your first offer! Now it's time to go back inside and present it.

PRESENTING THE OFFER

Always be tactful when presenting offers. If the homeowners told you how much they were hoping for and your offer is close to that number, then things are easy. But if you're offering significantly less than the amount they wanted or if you have no idea how much they want, presenting the offer can feel uncomfortable. Luckily, I have perfected a way of doing this that eliminates the discomfort and keeps the sellers liking you. It's crucial that the sellers continue to like you. The odds are good that they will say no today but agree to sell a few weeks or months later, after diligent follow-up on your part. Following up is much tougher, sometimes impossible, if they don't like you.

When you return from your car, open with, "Well, I have good news and bad news. The good news is the offer came out higher than I expected. The bad news is that it's still less than you were hoping to get." At this point, you're holding the contract in your hands, but do not give it to them or show them the amount. Pause, and remain quiet for a moment. This is tough to do, but it's important that you let them speak next. They will ask you how much you'll pay. Don't tell them. Not yet, anyway. Instead, discuss alternatives they might consider. "You can always just renovate it yourself," you might suggest. "It will only cost around $25,000, and you'll make more money when you sell." Ask if they've considered keeping the house as a rental. "If you hang on for another five years or so, until the market improves, you can definitely get more money."

This approach accomplishes several things at once. First of all, you are keeping your rapport alive and not pitting them against you—you're still on their side. Second, you are not being pushy. They will never feel like you are pressuring them. In fact, the opposite will be true. You're apprising them of all of their options, not presenting a sale to you as their best or only course. People appreciate this. It shows that you are not just looking out for yourself.

Continue taking this tack until they are practically begging you to give them the number. At this point you'll shrug or sigh. "I don't even want to tell you, because it's lower than you wanted, and I don't want you guys to be mad at me." They will generally promise not to get mad if only you'll tell them. Now, and not before, you can tell them the number. Watch their reactions as you give it. Usually, because of all of the buildup and your hemming and hawing, your offer will actually be higher than expected. You'll probably notice some relief on their faces, and if that's the case, they're ready to consider the deal.

Sometimes sellers will want to haggle with you on the spot. Maybe you offered $67,300, and their threshold is $70,000. They'll ask if you can boost the offer by a few thousand. I never agree to even a minor adjustment in price right away. If their counteroffer is close to mine, a number that I know will work for me, and I want to leave the house with a contract, I'll ask them to hang on while I call my boss to discuss it. I return to the car for ten minutes and return with a reason why I can make the new number work. My boss says if we can sell the house without replacing this roof or removing that tree, the new number is doable. Remember, you've given the impression that the offer you presented was scientifically computed—in fact, it was—and immediately altering it can make sellers think you were trying to take advantage of them. Well, if he can immediately raise the price by $3,000, why didn't he offer that higher number to start with? How much more might he be able to raise it? By calling your boss—even if you don't have one—and coming up with a specific reason for accepting the new number, you give the impression that you're straining to make the deal work. The original offer was rock solid, but here's a workaround, thanks to my extra effort and my boss's creativity, which might still allow us to make this happen.

ACTION PLAN

- Be confident on the phone, but don't answer questions you don't know the answer to.

- Make appointments as often and as soon as possible.

- Obtain background info on properties by utilizing MLS listings, websites (Trulia, Zillow, etc.), and tax records.

- Compare the property with other similar properties in the area.

- Build rapport with sellers and discover their motivations for selling.

- Tour the home and complete a RAW form to calculate repair costs.

- Determine your offer by considering the RAW form, ARV, and comparable properties.

- Build anticipation when presenting the offer.

 **CHAPTER 7**

SEALING THE DEAL

Finding deals, as I've pointed out, is the key to making money in this business. It's also your greatest challenge. If you've managed to make the phone ring, to set appointments, and to present well-formulated offers, the hardest work is done. In this chapter, I'll walk you through what to do when sellers respond to an offer. This is a comparatively simple step, so simple that most real estate books spend little or no time on it. There are only two options here, both obvious—sellers say yes, or they say no. But like lots of simple endeavors—what could be simpler than, say, singing?—there is an art to responding to sellers intelligently and with nuance, in ways that give you the best chance of sealing the deal and maximizing profit. As with all parts of this business, my goal is to hold your hand every step of the way through each of these two possible scenarios. Some of the advice I'm about to give might seem unconventional or too miniscule to matter, but trust me, attention to these details can mean the difference between sealing the deal or watching it fall apart, earning $20,000 on a house or earning $30,000, doing $120,000 worth of business next year or $180,000.

UH-OH, THEY SAID NO!

If your prospective seller declines your offer, you shouldn't freak out. In fact, you shouldn't even be surprised. Most sellers say no—at least, initially. Remember, your offer is probably 50 percent below the price they expected. This is a numbers game and a people business. Do not get discouraged. All is not lost, and your work is not done. First of all, to maintain the rapport you've built with the sellers, help them explore their other options. These might include renovating the house themselves, selling through an agent, doing a short sale, etc.

It might seem counterintuitive to help someone who just turned you down with options that don't include you, but you have to take the long view here. The rapport you've built and the due diligence you've done are investments that shouldn't be tossed away simply because an offer is initially declined. For starters, many sellers know other homeowners in circumstances like theirs, and if you've established good chemistry, they might send these referrals your way. Referrals are the best leads, and over the years I've had a lot of new customers referred to me by sellers who said no or who initially said no.

I keep saying "initially" here because nearly one-third of my purchases have come from sellers who declined my offer at the first appointment. That's a massive amount of business. Sellers often have unrealistic expectations or simply don't believe what you're telling them. In such cases, they'll often change their minds after they've had time to do some research, to talk to others, or simply to process the number you gave them. In real estate, *no* doesn't always mean *no*, if you're patient. This is why I've spent so much time emphasizing rapport. You need to stay on the homeowners' radar and make yourself as pleasant and helpful as possible. As I write this, one of my scheduled closings this month is for a house where the seller declined my offer more than a year and a half ago.

After you get over the fact that you were turned down and go over some other options with the sellers, you will leave the appointment. Before you drive away, though, sit in your car for a few minutes, and jot down as many notes as you can. These notes are not about the house—you already have those—these are about the sellers. Record their kids' names, sports they like, vacations they've taken, the hobby you discussed with them, the pets they gushed over, the sick parent they worried about, etc. Whatever details popped up in your conversation are key to your follow-up. You heard me right: follow-up! You must follow up even on the *nos*—especially on the *nos*.

With your bruised ego thoroughly in check, send them a thank-you card for taking the time to meet with you and show you their home. These cards should be personalized and sincere. The system I've developed over the years is to have photo cards made of myself involved in various activities. I have pics of myself fishing, traveling with my family, driving a sports car, attending baseball games, etc. These are all real hobbies of mine. I don't fabricate interests to force a connection (that would feel phony), but when sending a note to the sellers, I pick the card that best relates to the rapport I've built with them and handwrite my comments inside. They typically go something like this:

Thank you for meeting with me today. I enjoyed talking with you about your [mention topic from notes]. Good luck with the sale of your house. Please let me know if there's anything else that I can assist you with.

Call the sellers a week later to check in and see how things are going and then again a month after that. Continue to call until they either tell you to stop or tell you they have sold the house. Believe me, this is not a waste of time. Simple follow-up today means 30 percent more buys next year.

UH-OH, THEY SAID YES!

If the sellers accept your offer, you've done your job properly, and they have a realistic view of the market and their situation. Congrats, but remember, there is still time to screw it up. Don't buy that celebratory bottle of Dom just yet. After the sellers say yes, you will be working together for another couple of weeks. It's vital that you explain the process to them clearly so that no one gets upset. First of all, whichever strategy you're pursing (wholesaling, rehabbing, or renting), you'll need to sign a contract. I have included a copy of my basic contract in Appendix B. It has space for standard information, such as the sellers' names and the property address, as well as the price you agreed to and the closing date.

The "closing," sometimes also called the "settlement," or "settlement day," is when the property is legally transferred from the sellers to the buyer. If you've ever bought a house or condo, you're familiar with this process. You might have had an attorney present when you closed on your house. One or more real estate agents might have been there, and a representative of a title company probably assisted with legal documents and the loan transfer. If you plan on rehabbing the property yourself or holding onto it as a rental, you will close on it. If you're wholesaling the house, which is the strategy I recommend as you're starting out, you will not actually close on it—*your buyer* will. He or she will be bound by the same closing date, price, and other stipulations in the contract once you "assign it" (more on this later).

Whichever strategy you're pursuing, you must schedule a closing date. If you're wholesaling (assigning the house to an investor-buyer for a fee), you won't be at the closing—your buyer will—but proceed as if you will be there. As far as the sellers are concerned, you are a buyer like any other. This might seem odd or even duplicitous if you're unfamiliar with the process, but it isn't. The sellers have agreed to a price and terms they're satisfied with, and it won't matter later whether the money comes out of your pocket or another buyer's, as long as the price and terms are met.

I recommend that you schedule the closing for thirty days from the date you sign the contract. This is the maximum amount of time I allow before a closing, but unless there are special circumstances, I use the maximum. If you're rehabbing the house yourself, or keeping it as a rental, thirty days gives you and the sellers plenty of time to prepare. If you're wholesaling and you've followed my system, thirty days also is more than enough time to find an investor-buyer. In fact, if you're maintaining a good buyers list, which we'll discuss in detail in chapter 8, and have done your homework, you'll find a buyer in three or four days. I never schedule a closing more than thirty days out, because, first of all, the sellers I work with feel some urgency and want to close quickly. Second of all, more than a month simply means more time for something to go wrong, and I want my deals to run smoothly.

Depending on the sellers' pain, however, I might schedule a closing for less than thirty days out. If the sellers want to make a deal because they need money right away, I could schedule a closing for as soon as a week from the time we sign a contract. The important thing is to be clear and not set unrealistic expectations. There are times we can close very quickly, within a few days, but there also are many variables we can't control, such as payoffs for the mortgage and judgments, if they exist. There might be a title issue from fifty years ago that needs to be cleared up. Anything can happen, and I want my sellers to be aware of possible bumps in the road so that they're never shocked later. Maintain the trust and rapport you've created every step of the way.

You should also establish the number of times you'll need access to the house before the closing date, especially if you are wholesaling, as I recommend. Wholesalers need to bring prospective buyers through the house, so you need to make sellers aware up front that you'll need access a number of times—I usually say two or three visits—before closing. Tell them you'll need to show the place to your contractor or lender. Do not surprise the sellers with visits from strangers at all hours. That's the easiest way to kill your rapport and reputation.

When sellers have accepted your offer, it's also important to choose your words wisely. Always err on the side of caution: under-promise and overdeliver. Keep your paperwork simple, without complicated wording or difficult legal jargon. This might seem like odd advice, but don't use the words "sign" or "contract" either. Erase them from your vocabulary. When people hear that they have to "sign a contract," their radar immediately goes up. They get nervous and start thinking that they should probably show everything to a lawyer or ask others for advice. Replace "sign the contract" with "approve the paperwork." That little change in wording will get you more on-the-spot contracts and avoid involving the entire family tree in the transaction. Everything you're doing is legal and scrupulous and aboveboard, but moving quickly, with minimal headaches, is important for your business model and your sellers' financial or psychological health. Keeping things streamlined is another win-win.

So you've met with the sellers, agreed on a price and a closing date, and signed a contract. Before you leave, as you're walking out the door, stop and solidify the deal. I always say something like this: "I want to make sure that you guys are comfortable and happy with this deal because once I turn this paperwork in to the attorney, you can't change your mind, and I can't change my mind. If you have any doubts, I will rip the paperwork up right now."

You want your sellers to realize that what they've just signed is real and binding. It's quite possible they'll later talk to someone who will offer more money for the house, but by then it will be too late. I want them to know this up front. I seal the deal before leaving the house, and sellers understand that I will hold them to the contract.

ACTION PLAN

- Maintain rapport with sellers who said no by offering to help explore other options.

- Follow up with sellers who declined your offer.

- Schedule the closing date thirty days from the date the contract was signed.

- Secure access to the house before closing so prospective buyers can see the house.

- Avoid legal jargon when signing a contract.

 CHAPTER 8

QUICK FLIPS: WHOLESALING

Once the sellers of a house have agreed to your offer and signed a contract, you have several options, as covered in our overview of investment strategies in chapter 4. Because you have a contract, you're past the point of "bird-dogging," finding a deal and referring it to another investor for a fee. As I said in chapter 4, bird-dogging involves the lowest risk but also the lowest profit, and I don't recommend it, not even for beginners, unless you're completely risk-averse or a special situation makes this a good option (you're a mail carrier, for instance, who sees lots of potential deals on your daily route, but you do not want to invest personally).

After you have a contract, two of your options, both touched on in chapter 4, are "flipping" the house—rehabbing it and then selling it for a higher price—or keeping it in your portfolio as a rental. As I've said, I don't recommend you try either of these options straight out of the gate. Rehabbing is an involved, risky process that requires borrowing. Various circumstances might make it a good option for you, as I'll discuss in chapter 10, but even if rehabbing is your ticket, I don't recommend you try it until you've gotten a feel for the business. I am a big fan of rentals, and I would advise you to assemble a rental portfolio gradually over time because it's a great way to create a steady income stream and build long-term wealth. Like rehabbing, though, acquiring rentals means assuming debt, and you should avoid borrowing, even for short periods, while you're learning this business. Once you're comfortable and have built up some cash reserves (I'll get more specific about this in chapter 9, on rentals), you can begin picking up rentals as the right properties present themselves.

The final and, in my opinion, best option once you have a signed contract for a house is to wholesale it. This is where I shine—by far my favorite part of real estate. In wholesaling, as we mentioned in chapter 4, you put a house under contract for a price that's *very* below market and then sell it below market to another investor, who will either rehab it to sell or keep it as a rental. Why do I consider this the best and easiest strategy for investors, new or seasoned? I average $19,000 on my wholesale deals, but I have made as much as $105,000 wholesaling a single house—all without borrowing or risking any of my own money. As you get a feel for your market and your buyers' habits and preferences, wholesaling gets simpler and simpler, but the process is fairly straightforward from the word go. It's the ideal way to begin your career as a real estate investor and a great strategy to try if you've been pursuing riskier and more difficult routes in the business.

I gave you the broad outlines of wholesaling in chapter 4, but let's review. A typical wholesale deal goes like this:

1. Use marketing to find motivated sellers (covered in chapter 5).

2. Go on appointments and lock up a deal (covered in chapters 6 and 7).

3. Market that deal to your investor list.

4. Go to a closing/assignment.

5. Pick up a check the day after your buyer closes.

We'll cover steps 3, 4, and 5 in this chapter.

I can already hear you thinking, *How can I "lock up" a deal if I do not yet have a buyer?* What happens if I can't find a buyer for the house? How will I fund my buy? Relax. The process is simple, with no borrowing and very little risk, and I'm going to walk you through every step of it. You begin a wholesale deal just like any other, but once you have a contract in hand, instead of lining up contractors and financing, you line up buyers. You will assign the contract to one of these buyers for a fee, so in essence you are "flipping" the contract instead of flipping the house. You're acting as a middleman, which is why you don't need to borrow or use any of your own money to do the deal. I will go over building a buyers list later, but for now let's assume you have many buyers on your list.

FIGURING A SALES PRICE

The first order of business is to make sure your numbers are accurate. No one likes shaky numbers, and being off on your estimates is sure to irk the buyers whose confidence you want to win, especially early on. Buyers who know they can trust your numbers will take you seriously and will be much more likely to move on your deals. Review chapter 6, "Fielding Calls and Presenting Offers," to refresh your memory on how to figure out the house's after-repair value (ARV) and how to use the repair analysis worksheet (RAW) to figure renovation costs. Those elements are key in computing the price you offer sellers for their house, and they're also key in figuring out the price you'll offer it to your buyers for. The difference between the sellers' price and your buyer's—minus some other costs we'll cover shortly—constitutes your profit. Clean numbers maximize your profit and build your reputation. Sloppy numbers eat profits and scare buyers away.

To figure the price that you will market the house to buyers for, first take the house's after-repair value, or ARV, which you figured using comparable sales and the other methods discussed in chapter 6. Remember, we always buy using the low comps and sell using the high comps. Using techniques explained in that same chapter, you completed a RAW form to compute the cost of repairs needed to get the house in good shape—up to its ARV. The estimate for repairs doesn't need to be exact, but you can't afford for it to be way off the mark. Always be careful and thorough when figuring the RAW. Telling buyers a house needs $25,000 worth of renovation when it needs $50,000 will knock you off their radar whether or not they go for the deal. Now, subtract the total cost of repairs on the RAW from the ARV. This accounts for the money your buyers will have to spend rehabbing the house before they can market it.

Your buyers will have other costs, too, that you will build into the price you give them in order to make the deal work. From the number you just calculated, subtract a 6 percent real estate commission—the usual fee that real estate agents charge for marketing a home. Next, subtract 4 percent for assistance with closing costs. Closing costs, as you know if you've ever bought or sold property, include things like a title search fee, a recording fee, and a survey fee. The particulars don't matter, only the amount you'll deduct—4 percent. Next, subtract 6 percent for carrying costs. "Carrying costs" are the expenses related to holding a property for some period of time—things like utilities, home insurance, property taxes, and funding. Again, the particulars don't matter here as much as the overall amount you'll subtract. Finally, deduct the amount of profit your buyer needs for the deal to work. Remember, in wholesaling we buy very low and sell low because we're always leaving some profit on the table, or meat on the bone, for the next guy. How much? In my area, it's about $30,000 for the average deal. You'll have to get a feel for this in your market.

The house in the following example has an ARV of $200,000 and repair costs of $20,000. Here is how to calculate the price you would market it to your buyers for:

$200,000 - $20,000 (repair costs from RAW) = $180,000

$180,000 - $12,000 (6% agent commission) = $168,000

$168,000 - $8,000 (4% closing costs)   = $160,000

$160,000 - $12,000 (6% carrying costs)   = $148,000

$148,000 - $30,000 (buyer's profit)   = $118,000

Based on this example, you should be able to "sell" the house to someone on your buyers list for $118,000. I put "sell" in quotes because, as we'll explore in more depth later, you won't close on the property yourself while wholesaling but will transfer the contract to your buyer. Still, the calculations work as if you're buying and selling the house for a profit. Obviously, your purchase price—the amount on the contract you signed with the sellers—has to be lower than $118,000 or you won't make any money. Ideally, you would have paid around $100,000 for the house in our example, leaving $18,000 profit for yourself. If you signed a contract for much more than $108,000 with the sellers and your profit margin is under $10,000, you overpaid for the property.

You're probably eyeing that $30,000 line and thinking, *If there is still thirty grand left, why wouldn't I rehab the house and make that profit myself?* Well, good point, except that sometimes making $18,000 this week is a better proposition than making $50,000 six months from now. You can make the eighteen grand without borrowing any money and quickly lock it up in your bank account, while the fifty grand will remain on the table for half a year or more. A lot can happen in six months. Still, if you're dead set on going for all the money in the deal, then chapter 10, on rehabbing, is for you.

CHOICE BUYERS

You might be able to squeeze more profit out of a deal, however, depending on the particulars. The previous calculations can vary, which is why I said you must learn your buyers' habits. Some buyers use their own money, so they do not have "hard-money" carrying costs (I'll explain hard-money lending in chapter 11). Some buyers are agents themselves, so they save 3 percent on agents' commissions. Some buyers are contractors, so they can renovate for much less than the amount on your RAW form. Some people on your buyers list might have jobs and invest on the side, so they appreciate even a small amount of extra income. Knowing such factors and understanding your buyers' thought processes allows you to tailor deals to particular investors and to charge higher prices.

I consider these sorts of investors my "choice buyers," and I always give them first crack at my deals. They see the info on my houses before the rest of my list. What info? When presenting a deal to any buyer, you should include the home's address, the neighborhood or community name, the number of bedrooms and bathrooms, the square footage, and any pertinent features (two-car garage, finished basement, double lot, etc.). After this data, list the addresses, sales prices, and sales dates of recent comps (the comparable sales you used to determine the ARV, as discussed in chapter 6). I try to include comps that are no more than ninety days old, if possible.

All of this information should be presented in a clear, easy-to-read format, without the kind of gushing language you find in real estate ads. You're dealing with professionals, and they're interested in the numbers, not clichés and flowery descriptions. Never inflate your numbers to make a deal attractive—be completely honest or you'll destroy your reputation. Many books recommend that you share the ARV or rehab estimate you calculated with buyers. I don't. Your buyers are professionals and should do their own due diligence. If your numbers are off and the buyer loses money because of this, their hit becomes your fault.

Once I have my sales price locked down, I call or text my choice buyers before sending a general email blast to my full buyers list. This might not sound fair, but it works. It is simple psychology. People are wary of a deal if they think the entire investor community has already passed on it. Even with a terrific bargain, buyers might think, if it's such a good deal, why hasn't anyone else bought it? When I call or text my choice buyers, I use a little finesse. People have egos, and I don't want to bruise them. I try to figure out whom a particular house is best suited for and who will pay the highest price for it. I contact whomever that is and let that person know that I have called him or her first. I relay all of the information about the property and then give the person some time to do his or her own due diligence, consider the deal, and call me back. If the first person on the list isn't interested, I call number two and repeat the process. If one of these choice buyers sounds interested, I take that person to the next step of a walkthrough. Don't expect a commitment from a buyer before he or she has seen the house.

Showing the house is tricky. We don't tell the seller we're assigning the contract, yet we still need to get our buyer in. Typically, as I'm leaving a house after signing a contract, I let the sellers know I'm going to need to get into the house two or three more times. I tell them that I'll have to bring my contractor and my lender through to see the house. If you show up more than that, the sellers wonder why you keep parading people through the house. I don't show the home to just anyone who wants to see it, because I'm only getting a few more visits. Usually I only return once because when I call my buyers and give them the info on the house, I emphasize that they should do all their due diligence first. "I'm only going to show you the house," I say, "to verify that everything I told you was true." So, though a buyer obviously can't commit before he sees the property, he has to be essentially a "yes" before I'll take him in the house.

I recommend that you get a "no" from one choice buyer before moving on to the next. If you send your choice buyers deals, and they waste a day doing research only to express interest and be told, "Sorry, the house is already gone," they'll start to disregard your deals. Remember, this only applies to choice buyers—the people at the top of your list. The rest of the buyers list gets one email, sent in a single blast.

ASSIGNING VS. DOUBLE CLOSING

When a choice buyer wants the house, you will have to write up a contract. Now you have to decide whether you will "assign" the contract you wrote with the seller to the new buyer or "double close" on the property. Remember, in wholesaling you are flipping the contract. You are a middleman, transferring the contract you wrote with the seller to a new buyer, who will have to abide by the original terms. You don't have to borrow money or use your own, because you're simply transferring the deal to a new party, but—and this is important—there are two basic ways of doing this, each with advantages and disadvantages.

If you're working a deal that came from the MLS or a bank, perhaps a house in foreclosure, you will have to double close because those institutions won't allow an assignment. Otherwise, in dealing with homeowners, my preference is always to assign the contract. The standard contract I use, printed in chapter 6, looks like any other, though minor differences might exist among the documents used by various investors and from state to state. The contract includes a provision that says it's "assignable." When I've discussed what you can "sell" a house for, in terms of wholesaling, I'm talking about assigning the contract. When you find a buyer and agree on a price, you'll both sign a one-page assignment document saying that you contracted this particular property on a certain date and that you are now assigning your rights and interests in this property over to party X for Y amount of compensation. I've printed the assignment document I use in Appendix C, and you can find it online at www. scottsresources.com. Your payoff is the difference between what you contracted the house for—the offer your sellers accepted—and the price you calculated for your buyer ($118,000 in the example we used early in this chapter). If you contracted with the sellers of the house in our example for $100,000, the "assignment fee" would be $118,000 minus $100,000, or $18,000. Your buyer is now bound by the closing date, price, and any other terms you agreed to with the sellers.

This sort of assignment is perfectly legal and normal, and it doesn't affect what the sellers accepted in any way. If they agreed to sell for $100,000, with a closing on March 15, and to have me cover the closing costs, all of this will still hold. There will be a different buyer, and I'll make eighteen grand on the deal, but that doesn't affect the sellers. In fact, because they're getting everything agreed to and the contract allows for an assignment, there is no need to inform the sellers that you're assigning the contract.

A double closing is more complex than an assignment. Just as the name implies, in this scenario you close on the property twice—

first with the sellers and then, immediately after, with your buyer. There will be two sets of closing documents, and you do the closings "at the same table," as we say. You might not literally do them at the same table, but you get the idea—they are back to back. You will have a second contract with your buyer and a closing scheduled with him for the same day you're closing with the sellers. How do you fund the first closing? You don't—your buyer does. You must use an attorney for a double closing. He or she will have a note drawn up from your buyer to you for the total amount you need to bring to your buy. You'll use this to purchase the house at the first closing. At the second closing, when you sell, a line item on the HUD-1 Settlement Statement will return this money to your buyer. HUD stands for the US Department of Housing and Urban Development, and the HUD-1 form is a standard document used in home sales to itemize services and fees involved in the transaction.

There is nothing illegal about this process as long as you're doing a cash deal. If your buyer is using a bank or lender, he won't be allowed to loan you the money for the buy and you'll have to fund the deal yourself. Don't worry, this isn't too complicated or expensive. There are easy ways to fund this sort of deal that will probably cost you around $1,000 for the day. This kind of quick and easy financing is well worth the price, and I'll go over how to arrange it in chapter 11, on financing.

The reason I prefer to assign the contract rather than to double close it is that, with an assignment, I pay no fees. I simply get a check for the full amount of the assignment fee. It's a very simple process. If I double close, I have to pay the attorney's fees as well as recording fees and transfer taxes. This could cost me a $1,000 or more. The only time I choose to double close is if I am earning a huge fee and I am afraid my buyer will freak out if he sees just how much

I'm making. With a double closing, the buyer's info and seller's info are kept separate, so neither sees how much I'm making. My profit shouldn't matter if the deal is good for the buyer, and in many cases the investors don't care, but if I'm nervous about how they might react, I will gladly pay the $1,000 or so to pick up my huge fee.

What about your sellers? Are they going to freak out if they see that you are buying their house for a low price and then selling it the same day for twenty or thirty grand more? You bet they will! Before I knew better, I used to double close everything for this very reason. I spent sixty to a hundred grand a year just to spare sellers' feelings. It was crazy. Then a lawyer I knew taught me about using a "seller-side only HUD," a version of the HUD-1 Settlement Statement mentioned previously. Just as the name implies, when you use a seller-side HUD form at the closing, it includes only the information pertaining to the sellers. If I earn a $50,000 assignment fee, that's on the buyer's side and has no bearing on the sellers. They don't need to see it. Remember this approach. If you take nothing else from the book, this one strategy, which took me years to discover, will save you thousands of dollars.

Now that you have a feel for how to transfer a contract in wholesaling, let's return to our discussion of buyers. If none of your choice buyers wants a house you've put under contract, then it is time to market it to your entire investor list. Be ready for very different responses than those you received from your choice buyers. Your larger investor list will have hundreds if not thousands of investors, many of whom have never bought a house. Many will want to call you, see the property, and crunch the numbers, but only a few will be serious. That's fine. You only need one buyer, but this is a numbers game. Building an extensive investor list is the difference between success and failure for wholesalers. I have had investors on my list for years who looked at everything but bought nothing until one day, bam, they did.

REGULARS

Inevitably, as a wholesaler, you will have a handful of regulars who you start to do most of your business with. It becomes tough after a while to distinguish who is doing whom a favor in these symbiotic relationships. Your buyers need deals and you provide deals, so they need you. But you need buyers, and they buy houses, so you need them. It's important to keep both sides of this equation in mind. Several years ago, I had a deal scheduled to close with one of my regulars. Just before closing, he began moaning and groaning about some closing cost that he was going to have to pay. It was written into the contract, but he hadn't seen it. Not my fault, I thought. We argued and argued over this item. I stood to make about $15,000 on the assignment fee, but he stood to make about $30,000 after renovating the house. A few days went by, and then I attended a "lunch and learn" seminar, part of a series on business practices. This particular session, about customer service, focused on the lifetime value of customers.

Halfway through his talk, the speaker asked, "Do you know who your number-one customer is?" I considered the question and immediately thought of the guy I'd been arguing with. "What have you done for this customer lately?" the speaker asked. What I'd been wanting to do for that customer was tell him to take a hike and never approach him with another deal. But as the speaker emphasized the big picture, the lifetime value of a customer, and the importance of showing your best customers the ultimate in appreciation and service, I began to change my mind. In our business, customers like the one I was arguing with (over less than $1,000) can be worth hundreds of thousands of dollars, if not a million or more. I left that seminar with a new outlook, which I've maintained to this day. My buyers are my customers and should be treated as such. How much they make on my deals doesn't matter. In fact, the more they make, the better. That keeps them buying from me again and again. When I got home that day, I called my buyer's attorney and told him I'd pay the fee in question. I hung up and ordered a large box of Omaha Steaks to send to my buyer, along with a note thanking him for his business. That was many years ago, and he remains one of my top buyers.

I'll close our discussion of regulars with a pitfall that you should look out for—a trap that put me in a slump twice and hurts many of my coaching clients. Let's say you're doing well as a wholesaler, racking up five to ten deals a month. When you started out, you built a long buyers list and called nearly every investor on nearly every deal. After forty or fifty deals, of course, you started selling to the same five or six buyers. This makes your job easy. When you get a new deal, you make a few calls and bingo, the house sells. Life is good. Well, sure, until it isn't.

At some point, you'll see this pocket of investors as your only gauge of the market, and that can throw you off your game. You'll get a deal that makes sense to you, but your usual investors will all pass on it for one reason or another. You'll question your assessment and begin to second-guess whether or not it was really a deal—despite your careful analysis and due diligence. You'll either decide to rehab the house yourself or walk away from it, wondering what you did wrong.

The answer is, nothing.

Your five or six regular buyers are professional investors, just like you. They need to buy deep, just like you. They are following the market very closely, just like you. When you gradually stopped talking to the rest of the investors on your list and stopped adding new investors because you didn't need them, you lost touch with what the market would bear. Plenty of weekend warriors out there would be thrilled to make an extra $10,000, as opposed to the $30,000 the professionals demand. The part-timers might do only one or two deals a year, but your margins will be far greater when you sell to them. So, yes, maintain good relationships with those regular professionals, your choice buyers, but remember that they do not represent the entire market. Many other buyers on your list will pay more. Don't neglect them! Next time you're in a slump, try calling those high-profit buyers individually first (again, avoid the email blast early on, for the reasons we discussed early in this chapter). When you've exhausted them, turn to your professional investors. Be sure to reread this the next time poor response to a house makes you second-guess deals that seemed perfectly good.

BUILDING A BUYERS LIST

We skipped over how to build a buyers list early in this chapter because this task deserves special attention. I wanted to close this section on wholesaling with it because it's so vital to your project as a wholesaler. Building a buyers list is a lifelong process, not a one-time chore. The longer your list, the better equipped you will be as an investor. An extensive buyers list is the key to wholesaling properties quickly, for top dollar. Over time, a good list takes on a monetary value of its own. For instance, people often go through all of the hard work we discussed in the previous chapters and then bring me deals that they locked up simply because of my extensive list. They want me to wholesale a house for them because they know I have a long, quality list that brings quick results. For me, such offers are easy money. I mark up the house by five or ten grand, whatever I think the market will bear, and shoot the deal out to my contacts. I'll often have a solid response the same day and deposit $5,000 to $10,000 at the end of the month for a few minutes' work.

How big should your buyers list be? My list has more than two thousand names on it, but I sell probably to twenty. Even that's a slight exaggeration. Typically, when I contract a house, I know as I'm driving away who I'm selling it to because I know my buyers, I know their areas, I know what they'll pay. This makes the process easy. It's nice to have a long list, but you don't need a large number of cash buyers to do deals.

How do you build a good buyers list? I'll show you, but let me emphasize again that this is a task you must work on throughout your career. A good list can get stale if it isn't vigilantly maintained and developed, and if the list gets stale your business will sag. Remember, the money is in the list. Get as many people on there as you can, and get yourself on other peoples' lists, too. You can use Excel or another program to store your list, but my advice is to keep it simple. Some investors want everyone on their list to fill out a question-naire, detailing what types of property they buy, where they buy, how they typically fund deals, etc. Forget about all of that. Simply get the buyer's name, phone number, and email address. Always ask the buyer to spell his or her name—John can also be spelled Jon, and Smith can be Smyth. This might seem like a minor point, but misspelling the names of professional investors you don't know very well will make them wonder if you're equally careless when it comes to estimating house values or renovation costs.

Here are some great ways to start building your list:

- **Attend foreclosure auctions / tax sales.** It doesn't matter if you intend to buy or not, attending foreclosure auctions and tax sales will allow you to meet people who clearly are buying. Go to these sales, which are announced in your local paper. Bring your business cards, and pass them out. Meet as many people as you can, and get their cards or contact info. People never get mad about an investor who wants to send along deals asking for their contact info.

- **Call on others' ads.** Now that your brain is on real estate (remember chapter 3), you'll notice other investors' marketing as you drive around town, browse publications, watch TV, etc. Whenever you see a "We Buy Houses" bandit sign, lettered vehicle, or print ad, be sure to call and ask the investors for their info. They will be all too happy to give it to you.

- **Scour the MLS.** Look for rehabbed houses for sale in your local multiple listing service and in real estate ads, and find out who the sellers are. If this info isn't available, contact the agents for the sellers. They might be reluctant to provide the rehabbers' info, since they do not want to be cut out of the loop, but that's fine. Put the agent on your list. Agents love to bring their investors wholesale deals because they'll get the listings later.

- **Join investor groups.** When you attend local investor group meetings, as we discussed in chapter 3, go with a purpose. You want to learn and to meet people, but you should also get all the business cards you can and add them to your list.

- **Use Craigslist.** There are multiple ways to use Craigslist. You can call other investors who are offering their deals and get their contact info. Many of them will buy, too, if the right property comes along. You can also run ads seeking investors to opt into your deals. When you run an ad for a great deal, leave it active as long as possible, even after you have a contract on the house. When investors call, tell them that you have started working on a contract on that house but that they should give you their info, so you can contact them if it falls through. Add them to your list.

- **Visit rehabs in progress.** If you see a dumpster in a driveway or a roof popped off, stop in and introduce yourself. Explain that you're an investor and that you wholesale houses just like this one. Get the info for whoever is doing the job.

- **Build rapport with hard-money lenders.** Let them know about your deals. They'll often have buyers in mind, since these lenders finance them. They'll want to set you up with their customers because they'll do the lending and make money on the deal. In effect, this puts the lender to work for you.

- **Attend real estate investing seminars.** Every month, gurus will visit your town with a new twist on real estate investing. Thousands will flock to these seminars. So should you, in order to meet as many people as possible and get their contact info.

- **Peruse foreclosures.** Get in your car, and go browse the foreclosures listed for sale online or in your local paper. You'll usually run into other investors while you're looking at a house. Get their cards or contact info.

These are just some of the many possibilities. If your brain is truly on real estate, you'll come up with creative ideas of your own, too, to add to your buyers list. Keep potential buyers in the back of your mind as you go about your day, and you'll be amazed at the opportunities that arise for adding new names to the list. It doesn't cost anything to put one more name on—emails are free—so err on the side of being too inclusive. I have thousands of people on my list, and though it's true that most have never bought anything from me, you never know when they might get in the game.

ACTION PLAN

- Figure a sales price, and subtract various fees and commissions as necessary.

- Build a list of choice buyers, and give them clear, relevant info on your properties.

- Double close a contract if you're worried the seller will object at seeing your profit.

- Do your utmost to treat your regular customers well.

 C H A P T E R   9

SLOW FLIPS: RENTALS

I could write an entire book on rentals and probably will eventually, so stay tuned. In the meantime, because rentals are such an important part of your long-term strategy for building wealth, I want to share my general approach to buying the houses that I keep in my portfolio and rent out for steady income. Remember chapter 2, "Get a Life," where we visualized your ideal day and discussed the notion that the goal is not money but freedom? Well, rentals are the key to buying that freedom and living your days the way you want to. You can be the best rehabber or wholesaler on the planet, but the day your flipping stops, so does your income. That's not true with rentals. I once played craps with one of my lenders, a guy with millions of dollars and about eighty rentals that he owns free and clear. He was having a bad streak at the table but didn't seem to mind. "I could lose all of my money today, and on the first of the month I'll have eighty grand again," he said. I have often thought of that statement. In fact, it put me on the path to owning all of my rentals free and clear.

Rentals can feed you or they can eat you, as I often tell my students. They are the best and the worst of real estate. They're the best because they provide the steady income that allows you to get out of the game, or to play as much or as little as you want. They are the worst because, frankly, the learning curve is brutal. I have been doing this for twenty years and every now and then I still get taught a new lesson. Most books on rentals make them sound rosy—an effortless way to acquire wealth. I have a very different view. I love rentals, but after the housing crash, I am also wiser and no longer follow the conventional advice.

Most experts preach leverage, leverage, leverage when it comes to rentals. You do need leverage to acquire rentals, but I always look at borrowing as a necessary evil. Debt, as I've noted in previous chapters, is never a good thing and should always be dispensed with as soon as possible. I borrow to buy my rentals, but I pay off those loans as quickly as I can. This wasn't always the case, as I explained in chapter 1. Early in my career, I attended a real estate investment seminar where the speaker said, "Let's assume you have $100,000. You can buy one house for $100,000, or you can buy ten houses with $10,000 down each. With the first model, if you pay cash and the value goes up by 10 percent, you will have a gain of 10 percent. With the second, using leverage, the same 10 percent increase in value gives you a gain of 100 percent on your investment."

This example made perfect sense to me, and as I documented early in the book, I quickly built my strategy on that kind of leverage. In the end, I realized, I would have been far better off with that one house owned free and clear and a 10 percent return. The housing market crashed at the worst possible point for me, and that same leverage that can build your profits ten times faster works the same way in reverse. If I'd owned that one house valued at $100,000 free and clear and it fell in value to $80,000, I would have lost $20,000. With the leverage model, I would have lost all $100,000 and been upside down to the tune of another $100,000 (meaning the mortgages would have been worth that much more than the houses, a situation we also call "negative equity").

None of this matters much unless you are going to sell a rental. If you are holding properties and they are occupied and the cash is flowing, the market value is almost irrelevant. The part the speaker brushed over, however, was the reality of vacancies, truancy, repairs, and destructive tenants. I do not say this to scare you but to prepare you. Falling value is one thing. Values falling while growing numbers of tenants fall behind on their rent is another. It's easy to weather a downturn in the market if you own a number of your rentals free and clear. If you're highly leveraged, you'll have a tougher time making mortgage payments, and it's frighteningly easy to slide into foreclosure. After surviving the real estate crash that began in 2007, my strategy evolved. I now hold off on reaping the benefits of rentals so that I can pay them off as quickly as possible. My advice is, keep the debt minimal, postpone the profits, and then collect the rewards for the rest of your life.

This approach, as I said, is the opposite of what most experts preach. So is my advice on the types of properties you should buy. I buy at the top of the low end. This is where I get the best returns (I could get even better returns, in theory, at the bottom of the low end, but I draw the line where I feel concerned for my safety). I've read several books that advise readers not to buy any rental that they would not want to live in. I couldn't disagree more. I have about seventy rentals and would only live in one of those units—a prior home I actually did live in and decided to keep when I moved. I am in this business to turn a profit, and the biggest profits are in the lower-end homes.

The problem with houses at the top of the low end, compared to higher-value homes, is that they tend to suffer higher tenant turnover and more headaches. We'll address ways to minimize those problems shortly, but for now let's focus on what I see as the sweet spot in the market. For $100,000 in my area, I can buy a house that would bring in about $1,000 a month in rent, or I can buy three properties at the top of the low end for $33,000 each and rent them for $750 a month each. The rents in the second scenario total $2,250—a huge difference that would be well worth some extra headaches short term. In the seriously distressed areas I avoid, you could probably buy four houses for $25,000 each and rent them at $700 for a total of $2,800, but the difference in income is not worth the stress and safety risks for me. I have friends who work exclusively in that space and do very well. This is a personal decision you'll have to make based on your comfort level.

As with wholesaling and rehabbing, you should get a feel for your local market and do careful due diligence before buying a house to keep in your rental portfolio. In terms of finding and purchasing the house, everything we covered in chapters 5, 6, and 7 applies. You want to look for a deal and buy as low as possible, since this will maximize your return. Find comparable properties to figure the ARV, fill out a RAW form in order to deduct the cost of needed repairs, and present your offer just as you would if you planned on wholesaling or rehabbing the house.

Unlike in wholesaling, however, you will close on this property, hold it, and rent it out to tenants. Analyzing a potential rental is different because you also need to assess likely cash flow. This is similar to figuring out the market value of a house. Here, you also use comparables, but the comps are rentals similar to the property you're considering. Websites that list rentals in your area can help, as can your real estate agent, but one tried-and-true method I recommend is simply driving around the immediate area and calling on rental signs for similar properties. Look for places with the same number of bedrooms and bathrooms, similar square footage, and features. How much is your type of house renting for?

Once you establish how much you can expect in monthly rent, deduct from this amount the likely cost of vacancies and repairs. I recommend that you subtract at least 10 percent for vacancy and 15 percent for repairs. This might sound high, but trust me, in lower-end homes it's about right. Next, subtract 10 percent for management fees. Even if you plan on managing the house yourself, factor this fee in just in case the situation changes. You should also estimate how much you'll pay in taxes and insurance—the amount the sellers paid last year will be a good gauge (for my average house, it's about $100 a month). Subtract these amounts from the estimated monthly rent. The amount you're left with must be enough to cover your monthly debt service, whether you borrowed from a bank or another source.

Here's an analysis of a potential rental house:

$875 expected rent

- $87.50 (10% for vacancies)

- $131.25 (15% for repairs)

- $87.50 (10% for management fees)

- $100 (taxes and insurance, based on last year)

$468.75 (left for debt service and profit)

If the final amount covers your debt service, you can hold onto the house as a rental and make it work financially. As I've said repeatedly, however, do not start buying and holding onto rentals your first month out. Wait until you've done a few deals, and most important—wait until you have *at least* the cash equivalent of three months of debt service on reserve. Let me repeat, after you have figured out your likely monthly mortgage payment on a rental, do not buy it unless you have, minimally, three months of payments in cash on reserve. Rentals are risky and lots can go wrong for landlords, so proceed cautiously.

How do you know what your debt service will be? That depends on how you finance your rentals. Several options are available. If you have a job, excellent credit, and cash to put down, you can simply go to a bank and get a mortgage. I won't focus on that method, because many readers already are familiar with it from buying homes of their own and because I have operated without banks since the housing bust in '08. Today, I use three primary strategies for financing rentals: owner financing, lease options, and short-term private mortgages. I will cover these in chapter 11, "Creative Financing."

Whatever form of financing you use, I recommend that you keep the term as short as possible. Cover your payments, taxes, and insurance, and trade monthly profits today for peace of mind tomorrow by paying off your loans quickly. Another reason I like buying at the top of the low end of the market is that it allows me to pursue what I call "the slow flip." Housing prices vary from market to market, but in my area, I pick up homes at the top of the low end for around $30,000, as I said. I use private money (we'll also cover this in chapter 11), pay 12 percent interest, and amortize the loan over five years.

I don't make any money on a monthly basis while I'm making payments on these deals. My only concern is that the tenants' rent covers my debt payments, property taxes, and insurance. On a $30,000 mortgage amortized over five years at 12 percent, my payment is about $667. My average rent on that sort of house is about $875. I put nothing in my pocket, but the tenants' payment covers my debt, taxes, and insurance—and in five years I own the property free and clear. At that point, most of the rent becomes income for me. I can breathe easy, withstand vacancies or dips in the market, and with enough of these units in my portfolio, work as much or as little as I want.

If I buy houses at $50,000, my monthly payments rise to $1,000 or $1,100 a month, and I can't make the deals work. I can't break even. As I said, markets vary, but if you're pursuing this strategy, you can't be "upside down," not even by $50. To make a slow flip feasible, the tenants' monthly payment must cover all of your monthly expenses.

Once you close on your rental house, don't waste any time in making the needed repairs and putting it on the market. I have learned over the years that it's actually cheaper to paint and carpet a house at every turnover—not just when it appears to need it. A freshly painted and carpeted unit rents three times faster than one with older carpet and less-than-pristine walls, and the cost of that cosmetic renovation is lower than the cost of having the house sit vacant for months.

Speaking of repairs, tenants can drive you crazy, calling at all hours of the day and night. Apart from the routine plunging of toilets and shoveling of snow, physical upkeep on existing homes is expensive and time consuming—new roofs, furnaces, water heaters, pipes, etc. These sorts of headaches almost drove me out of rentals altogether before I found the "lease option," which I have now evolved into land contracts, a key piece of my slow-flip strategy. With land contracts or contracts for deed, my renters are technically not tenants but tenant-buyers who are purchasing the home. I buy a rental house for $30,000 and then set up tenant-buyers with long-term owner financing. I retain the title while they make payments over a specified term. Technically, I'm selling the house for $80,000 to $100,000, but the tenant-buyers rarely stay for the full term (the average length a homeowner stays in the same house in America is about six years). The people interested in these deals tend to have poor or no credit and can't get traditional bank loans. They give me a down payment of $3,000 to $5,000 and agree to monthly payments on a thirty-year loan. Every month, a portion of their payment is going to principal, just as if they'd gotten a bank loan.

The beauty of this arrangement is that I am no longer responsible for maintenance and repairs. During my orientation with my tenant-buyers, I emphasize that I'm nothing more than a finance company. They are completely responsible for repairs and can no more call me to fix a leak than they would call the bank if they'd purchased with a traditional mortgage. Some newbie investors worry, what if these tenant-buyers all decide to pay off the houses? That rarely happens, but if it does, everyone's happy. The tenants who had bad credit and couldn't qualify for a traditional mortgage found a way to buy a house. At least some of their monthly payment was applied to the cost of buying. You bought the house at wholesale for $30,000, paid it off in five years, and then sold it to them at retail for $80,000 to $100,000, with no agent's commission. And because the tenants are buyers, I eliminate the costs associated with management, repairs, and even vacancy. If they suddenly leave, a new down payment will more than cover whatever term the house sits vacant for. This is a game changer! I have tried many strategies to buy and operate rentals. I came to "the slow flip" through painful trial and error, and I would never do rentals any other way.

ACTION PLAN

- Pay off loans on rental properties as quick as you can.

- Consider whether you want to rent out a low-value or high-value property.

- Calculate your expected income based on rent, vacancies, repairs, fees, taxes, and insurance.

- Decide which financing strategy works best for you.

- Utilize long-term owner financing to avoid the hassles of repairs

CHAPTER 10

HOUSE BEAUTIFUL: REHABBING

People who love to rehab generally are into it because they love taking something ugly and making it pretty. That, in my opinion, is the best reason to rehab. Wholesaling, as I've pointed out, has fewer headaches, less risk, and a quicker (though smaller) return. If you're only investing for the money, there are many other ways to make solid returns, too—all of which carry less stress. My advice is to rehab because you love that process—picking out finishes, overseeing contractors, planning renovations—or find another strategy.

Flip This House is a great show, but it's entertainment, not reality. At the end of a segment, when they present the numbers and say, we bought this house for $100,000, put $50,000 into it, and sold it for $200,000, they leave out many costs—agent commissions, carrying costs, closing cost assistance. I like to do the math while watching, and frequently when investors say they made $50,000, it should actually be closer to $17,000. That's nothing to sneeze at, but it's a far cry from the $50,000 they claim. No one should feel like a failure for not living up to the show's unrealistic numbers.

If you've watched *Flip This House* and have paid attention to rehabs lately—if your brain is on real estate, as I recommended early in the book—you might have observed that two kinds of houses sell in this market: distressed houses and showroom-condition houses. Gone are the days when a rehabber could simply paint and carpet. Now, every rehabbed house gets gutted down to nothing and restored to mint condition—stainless steel appliances, granite counters, new flooring, brushed-nickel hinges, etc. The in-between houses, and houses with merely cosmetic rehabs, are tougher to market. The distressed house, because of its low price, actually will sell faster than the inventory in the middle quality-wise.

If you decide to take the plunge and rehab, I recommend that you always put up a sign that says "For Sale Soon: Completely Remodeled" with your phone number early on. Very few people use such signs, though they cost only about $40. I've sold only two properties off these signs, but my average rehab sale was around $200,000. With no agent commissions to worry about, that's $12,000 extra profit per house. I think $24,000 is a pretty good payoff for a $40 sign, even if I buy them for the rest of my life and never sell another home off one.

A much bigger cost—and the reason I got out of rehabbing—is contractors. The word "contractor" begins with "con" for a reason. There are plenty of good contractors, of course, but I've had my share of problematic ones, and so will you if you rehab. They can make or break you in this business. If you have good contractors, you'll likely see profits, and if you have bad ones, you'll leave the deal with a bill—potentially a large one.

How do you find good contractors? A referral from someone you trust, as always, is one of the best ways. Stopping at local job sites, which you're doing anyway as you look for buyers, also will put you in touch with contractors. Other investors can help, but there are problems with this method. Good contractors have limited time and manpower, and so many investors are reluctant to refer their contractors to others.

Check with the Better Business Bureau to see complaints lodged against contractors before hiring them, and always make sure that they are licensed, insured, and bonded. Get references—and call them! As I'll repeat in chapter 11, I was badly ripped off by a contractor once when I didn't bother to call his reference. I did later, after losing a small fortune, and the reference had as many problems with him as I did. The contractor had bet that I wouldn't bother to call, and he was right. To this day, that contractor uses me as a reference because I'm a known investor. Occasionally someone calls about him, and I offer my honest, extremely low opinion, but most of his prospects probably see my name, assume I'd say something nice, and never call. Don't make that mistake.

If despite your best efforts you hired a shoddy contractor, don't let that bad apple fester on your job. The longest days in your life as a rehabber are the ones between the point when you realize you need to get rid of a contractor and the point when you actually do it. I learned this the hard way with a contractor I discovered was lying to me. I should have fired him on that day, but of course this is tough to do. I was in the middle of a job, things were half-finished, and I had a tight timeline. I would have lost maybe $20,000 if I'd fired him on the spot, a big loss. Instead, I kept him on and later got screwed to the tune of almost $100,000.

If you do manage to hire good contractors, you can easily turn them into headaches by dumping too much money or too much work on them. I've had contractors who were working out well— until I gave them three houses at once to work on. The next month, my guy shows up in a new truck, saying he needs a fourth house so that he can finish the first three. Our contractors are regular working people, and when they suddenly get a check for $40,000 they think they're rich. They're tempted to overspend. The bigger companies, which we can't afford as small rehabbers, have bookkeepers on staff, but the small contractor might have trouble managing checks for $30,000 or $40,000. Big money up front also lowers incentive for small contractors. They feel as if they already got the profit from the job and are now working for free.

Here are some more tips for dealing with contractors that I learned the hard way over many years of rehabbing:

- **Start small.** Some contractors are excellent salespeople and will sell you on what a great job they'll do. No matter how good they sound, begin with that tile job in the bathroom or painting the living room. See how they do with this level of work before moving on to bigger items.

- **Time will promote or expose contractors.** If the contractors' main skill resides in sales pitches, time will reveal this. If they are honest and have real ability, time will show this, too.

- **Hire the guy who does the work!** We all screw up on this. You don't need a general contractor, or GC, at least not when you're doing one or two rehabs at a time. When you hire a GC (a guy who's going to hire a guy to do the work) you increase your costs.

- **Hire specialists only.** Avoid the jack of all trades! If you hire a person to put in the roof, and he says, I can also paint the exterior and install your water heater, you got the wrong guy. Hire electricians for the electric, plumbers for plumbing, flooring guys for floors, etc. They're not only better, they're cheaper. They have the right equipment, they know what they're doing, and they'll be in and out without screw-ups.

- **Never let them get ahead of you.** When contractors request "draws," or payments, and want more money than the work that they've completed so far warrants, you'll lose by fronting funds. Pay as you go. A good contractor should have credit, so the excuse that he had to pay for X or Y up front is not valid.

- **Never reveal your budget.** Many rehabbers say the opposite, recommending you state exactly what you'll pay. I don't, because for starters, the contractor's rate might be less than you were willing to pay. Why tell him you'll spend $4,000 if he was ready to charge $3,000? Second, you don't want the contractor to simply go along to placate you. If you say the work has to be done for $20,000, and he thought it would cost $30,000, you might have made a mistake and it can't be done for $20,000. Now he's agreed to something he can't deliver in order to get the job, and an ugly situation develops.

- **Don't always go for the lowest price.** In keeping with the previous point, the lowest price isn't always the best one, especially if the contractor can't finish for the amount agreed to. I've said to contractors, well, this guy gave me price X, and they say, okay, he can have the job. It can't be done for that price. I take the lower bid, and sure enough, pay an even higher rate later.

- **Always get a detailed breakdown of work.** This is difficult. You can't just say "new kitchen." You need to itemize— how many cabinets, exactly which appliances, what type of flooring, which fixtures. Be specific, and put a price next to each item. Otherwise, there's room for interpretation and arguments.

- **Establish weekly draws.** Don't ever give a contractor a big check up front. Establish weekly draws, and inspect the work weekly. If you don't have time to inspect weekly, which I don't these days because I travel so much, don't do rehabs!

I could write an entire book about rehabbing. This chapter is only the tip of the iceberg, but so many people are interested in "flipping houses" these days, I wanted to give you some idea of what to expect, share some tips, and warn you of potential pitfalls. Rehabbing carries higher risk than many other types of investing, but the profits can be high, too. As I said at the start of this chapter, don't pursue this strategy unless it's a labor of love, and even then, get a feel for the industry before you attempt that first rehab.

ACTION PLAN

- Be cautious of bad contractors—the cost of rehiring contractors can be extensive.

- Don't overwork your contractors so they become dependent.

- Utilize specialists for various jobs.

- Find the right price (not always the lowest price) and get a breakdown of all the work to be done.

 CHAPTER 11

CREATIVE FINANCING

I'm a big fan of wholesaling, especially for those starting out in the industry, because no financing is required. You never have to borrow. In this chapter, I'll discuss how to finance two other types of deals: rehabs and rentals. Much of your ability to begin rehabbing or to assemble a rental portfolio, if you choose to pursue these strategies, comes from knowing how to finance such deals. No, you can't begin rehabbing houses with no money, but if you understand "hard-money lending," you can begin rehabbing with no money of your own. Likewise, owner financing allows you to pick up rentals without any of your own funds, and "private money" provides another easy source of funding for rentals. I'll explain each of these strategies, with the pros and cons, here.

FINANCING REHABS: HARD MONEY

"Hard money" is different from "private money," though they're both private in a sense. We obtain hard money from lenders who make short-term loans professionally. Lending is their business, so their rates and terms are quite expensive.

The first time that people hear hard-money rates quoted, they tend to think, *There's no way I would pay that.* That reaction is understandable, but using hard money is often the only way you can do a deal. Once you get over the sticker shock of how much hard money costs, take a deep breath and focus on the math. If you can pay this ridiculously high rate and still make a profit—and your only other choice is to not do the deal—who cares that these lenders charge exorbitant rates? Banks charge much lower rates, but unless you have sterling credit that you're willing to risk, and you don't mind long delays and many hoops, traditional lenders won't work for your rehabs. Once you're established, you might be able to get lines of credit from a bank and borrow at much lower rates. I have friends who have millions in lines of credit with banks and get interest rates of 2 or 3 percent. That's great for them, but if you're starting out in rehabbing, hard money is the way to go.

What's a typical interest rate? Are you sitting down?

The average is around 15 percent, but that's not the expensive part, since the terms are so short. Hard-money lenders make most of their profit on points. You're probably familiar with "points," or "discount points," if you've ever bought a home. Each point equals one percent of the loan amount, and you can think of it as prepaid interest, a fee added immediately when you get a loan. Hard-money loans might carry anywhere from three to eight points, but five points at 15 percent with a six-month term is fairly typical.

This means that if I borrow $100,000, on day one of the loan I owe $105,000, and I'm paying 15 percent interest on $105,000. The 15 percent interest is figured annually, but I always borrow hard money for a term of six months, so I figure the total loan expense at 12.5 percent. This includes the 7.5 percent in interest I'll pay (a 15 percent *annual* rate means I pay half that amount, or 7.5 percent, for six months) plus five points, which is 5 percent of the loan amount ($5,000 on a $100,000 loan). I might pay less in interest if I get the house sold in three months, but I always figure six months just in case. I have found lenders with lower rates, but they want borrowers to get surveys and home inspections and clear other hurdles. I prefer to avoid the hassles and delays and pay the higher rates.

Sure, it's hard to swallow that the lender who spends thirty seconds writing a check is making nearly as much as you after your months of hard work. I learned early on in this business, however, that worrying about how much the next guy makes means cutting off your nose to spite your face. In fact, you want your hard-money lenders to make money on your deals—lots of it—so that they're thrilled to keep doing business with you. Borrowing from a bank requires credit, collateral, and significant risk. Borrowing from a hard-money lender requires only a house that meets the lender's standards. The house gets approved, not you. The hard-money guys are happy to take this bet because, if you've followed my formula, you're borrowing on a house that you bought wholesale for, say, $40,000, and it's worth perhaps $100,000 retail. They profit handsomely if you can't pay them back.

Most hard-money lenders will loan 65 to 70 percent of a house's after-repair value, so you have to be buying a true deal and making a low enough offer, according to my system, for this kind of loan to work (see chapter 6 on presenting offers). If hard-money lenders won't back your deal, it's probably not profitable, and you should rethink it. Their assessment acts as a check on your numbers, which is especially helpful when you're starting out. Think of the lender as a second set of eyes proofing your math.

Where do you find hard-money lenders? Investment clubs are a good place to start. You can also go to other job sites and see who funded those rehabs. Ask agents you're friendly with. You can search for "hard-money lenders" online and find national companies that make these loans, but you'll have more hoops to jump through, so I recommend you find local lenders.

Because the hard-money guys are not banks, you might encounter a minor hurdle in using them. Some banks or agents you're dealing with might require a "proof of funds" letter when you're doing a deal. This is a dilemma because you don't technically have any funds yet, even though you might know that you can close and have hard money lined up. You can just type a simple letter on white paper with no letterhead. Just be sure to include the lender's name and the amount being loaned and the property address. This actually works, partly because the people approving such letters are bureaucrats who simply need to check boxes—yes, we received this letter. No one is scrutinizing it too closely.

Hard money is the most expensive funding you'll get, but if you're in the industry long enough, you'll appreciate how easy the best hard-money lenders are to deal with. Yes, it's pricey, but if the deal is right, it's well worth it.

PROS OF USING HARD MONEY

- easy to get, no credit check—the house qualifies, not you

- can close in as little as a week, sometimes a day

- allows scaling up with no cap on liquid funds—you can do as many deals as you want at one time

CONS OF USING HARD MONEY

- expensive

FINANCING RENTALS

Private Money

The professionals loaning hard money do it as a business, so they have set rates and terms. Private-money lenders are not pros, just people who would like to earn more than the low rates that banks pay on the funds in their accounts (less than 1 percent as I write this).

This sort of lending must be private. It's illegal for you to publicly raise money for deals—on TV commercials or online, for instance—without creating a "private placement memorandum." Such a document allows you to start a fund that people invest in, creating a pool of money you can use to do deals—a complex undertaking I tried once and don't recommend. As long as you're keeping things private, anyone with some spare dough can become your private-money lender. Your rich cousin Joe is tired of earning 1 percent at the bank? He can lend that money out for your rehabs and earn 5 to 12 percent.

I typically pay 12 percent to my private lenders. Some people think that's crazy, but again, I don't care how much profit the lender sees, as long as I make money. Unlike hard-money lenders, who fund rehabs, private-money lenders usually fund rentals. The interest rates and terms of these loans are negotiable. I usually take private money for a five-year term, since in the slow-flip system, I'm on a fast track to pay off my rentals as quickly as possible. But then again, I like stress. You might be more comfortable with a longer term, say seven years, which is what I usually recommend to students.

Who are these mysterious lenders? There are droves of people out there with half a million dollars, a million, three million sitting in banks, and they're frustrated by low returns. You might think they would fear the risk, but real estate eases fear, especially discounted real estate, because of the built-in collateral. If you say to a lender, "I want to borrow money for the house I'm moving into, and I'm paying $100,000 for it because it's worth $100,000 today," that's a risky proposition. If through your hard work, however, you're buying a house worth $100,000 for $40,000, that's a much safer bet. My lenders know that after I do all of the work to find and lock up a deal, they'll make 12 percent if I don't default. If I do default, they get a $100,000 house for $40,000. It's almost a no-lose situation for a private lender.

You must use an attorney with a private-money lender. He or she will establish the same "note and deed of trust" against the property that a bank would. This document ensures that if you default, the private lender can foreclose just as a bank would. The lender then would own the property or take the proceeds after it was sold at auction. He's completely secure as long as your attorney has drawn up the proper paperwork. Simply send your lawyer the terms you negotiated with the lender: *I'm borrowing $30,000 at 12 percent for five years from Joe Smith.* The attorney handles it from there, and you sign at closing.

Where can you find private money? Here are some suggestions:

- Start with family and friends, enthusiastically!

- Network. The money's out there, so let everyone know what you do.

- Build relationships. Many who say no now will say yes in two or three years.

- Make a "brag book." Photograph all houses before and after rehabbing them, list specs on your completed projects, and document the numbers on deals to show you're for real.

- Hone your "elevator pitch," a concise version of what you do, for presentations.

Since private-money investors are ordinary people you could find anywhere, approaching them requires a little finesse. Keep it positive and avoid fear, which is the motivation behind a surprisingly high number of decisions in our lives. Never ask people if *they* want to lend you money. Ask if they know anyone who would be interested in earning a return of 8 to 11 percent. If they're interested, they'll ask about the investment, but they'll feel better about doing so. They won't be defensive, because you didn't pitch them. The minute you ask for money, walls go up. Approaching potential lenders in this way makes the courtship easier for you, too, since you're not pitching directly.

Approach potential lenders with the right attitude. You're never asking for money, you're always offering an opportunity. Say, "Do you know anyone who wants to make X amount of return," not, "Do you know anyone who wants to loan me money?" This is a big difference, believe me, not just a trick in wording.

PROS OF PRIVATE MONEY

- longer terms possible—five years or seven, depending on your comfort level
- lower rates—you negotiate them with a private party
- can be used for rentals (hard money can't)

CONS OF PRIVATE MONEY

- takes time and work to raise—these lenders aren't in the phone book

- harder to raise on early deals, when you don't have a track record

Owner Financing

Sometimes I can fund a rental house with even lower rates—or none—through owner financing. In this slow-flip scenario, the seller acts as a lender, extending credit to me, the buyer, but with no down payment on my end. We both sign a promissory note and record a mortgage or deed of trust, and I pay the loan back to the seller with monthly payments over a specified term. The terms tend to be shorter than those of typical bank loans—sellers don't want to wait the thirty years that institutions will—and the rates tend to be lower. I usually go for a ten-year term with owner financing, which is not exactly private money but similar.

This arrangement works well with sellers who don't have a money issue but are fixated on a particular sales price. If this is the case, I can often get them to finance the deal—sometimes at 0 percent. I have several deals now where I'm at 0 percent because the sellers were so hung up on getting a certain price, they were willing to finance in order to get it. You must do the math for both scenarios on such deals. I offered $50,000 for one house. The sellers were hung up at $60,000, but by getting them to finance the sale at 0 percent, it actually cost me less than if I'd bought the house at $40,000 financed with private money. This is a great scenario because when you make a $600 payment, $600 comes off the principal. With traditional financing, if you pay $600, maybe $300 comes off the principal and $300 is interest.

Once we have a deal, I put tenant-buyers in the house with a lease option (see chapter 9, on rentals) and collect a down payment, usually in the neighborhood of $3,000 to $5,000. The tenants' rent covers my payments to the sellers and other incidentals, such as insurance and property taxes, and I'm on the road to slow-flipping another rental without using any of my own money.

PROS OF OWNER FINANCING

- often cheaper than other financing, even with a higher sales price

- requires none of your own money

- most or all of your payments come off principal

CONS OF OWNER FINANCING

- sellers sometimes confused by this arrangement

 **CHAPTER 12**

DEVELOPING YOUR SUCCESS TEAM

Many investors don't fully appreciate the importance of a strong, loyal, competent team in real estate investing. The more time and energy you put into building this team, the more successful you'll be. If you're learning the business, working with skilled professionals will be its own education. If you know what you're doing, working with reliable people takes work and worry off your plate and allows you to focus on the next deal. Cost is just one of the considerations here, so don't get too hung up on it. Sometimes cheap gets pretty expensive by the end of the day.

Just as you shouldn't underestimate the importance of building your success team, however, you shouldn't make it so important that it stops you from moving forward. I've seen endless newbies get so fixated on developing their teams that they never reach the point of doing a deal. Selecting and vetting members of your team can become a full-time job rather than one important part of the process. Think of building this team as a lifelong process. It's important but never quite complete. Take it seriously, but at the same time don't look for perfection or let it hold you back.

Now let's explore who you'll need on your team and how to go about selecting them.

ATTORNEY

You will need a real estate attorney to handle your closings. Attorneys are critical members of success teams because they can make or break deals. A skilled attorney can save you a fortune over the years, and a careless one can cost you dearly. Start your search for the right person with referrals from the fellow investors you meet at your local real estate investor meetings. You need to develop a relationship with this attorney so that he or she won't charge you or start the clock every time you have a question. A lawyer will be more likely to do extra work for free if you're loyal and give him or her all of your business. On occasion, buyers or sellers insist on closing with their attorneys, but otherwise use yours and stay loyal.

INSURANCE AGENT

A good insurance agent can be critical to your cash flow. When I moved to Virginia I purchased car insurance through one of the big companies. Shortly after that, I started purchasing houses, so I naturally just went to the same agent. I got along great with this agent and trusted her. About twelve years and eighty rentals later, I was selling two fourplexes to an insurance agent who wanted a shot at my business. I gave him my info and took a quote only because he was my customer and I felt obligated. The results shocked me. My average policy at the time cost about $1,150 a year. The new guy could give the same coverage for $450. It was an expensive lesson. I transferred all of my policies, and since then I've gotten multiple quotes every year. I use the same guy and refer him often, but I still get the quotes to prevent another oversight that could cost me hundreds of thousands of dollars.

HARD-MONEY LENDERS

Hard-money lenders use their own funds to provide loans. Because it's their money, you usually don't have to jump through too many hoops to get funded, which means you can close quickly. Private lenders are key because they enable you to make offers with the confidence that you can actually close. I've had wholesale buyers back out on the day of closing, but because I could pick up the phone and quickly get a check for a hundred grand or more, I didn't lose those deals. Yes, you'll pay these lenders a higher rate, but the tradeoff is worth it. My lenders make good money off me, but I make good money—and have access to quick, hassle-free loans—because of the service they provide. Depending on where you live, you can probably find local hard-money lenders with a Google search, but again, I recommend you ask for referrals from fellow investors you trust.

CONTRACTORS

This is a tough one. I'm sorry to say that you'll probably always have to add contractors to your success team. Rarely do I meet an investor who has used the same contractor for twenty years. You can ask for referrals, but they're tough to get. Investors fear their crack contractors will have even less time for old customers as they get new ones. Check with the Better Business Bureau to make sure a contractor is reputable. Always make sure that they are licensed, insured, and bonded. Develop relationships with contractors in specific trades— plumbers, carpenters, electricians, etc.—so you'll know whom to call when specific problems arise. Get references and call them. Earlier, I mentioned getting ripped off by a contractor because I never called a reference—just the sort of carelessness he banked on. Don't make that mistake!

REAL ESTATE AGENT

You will need a real estate agent's help on multiple fronts. He or she will run comps for you, send you listed deals, submit offers, and list your retail houses for sale. Pick someone who's not only experienced, skilled, and professional but also someone you like. You'll work closely with your agent, so think of this relationship as a kind of marriage. Don't settle on the first agent you try, just as you wouldn't propose on your first date. Court several. Ask investor friends for recommendations. See who's doing a lot of business in your area, but make sure your potential agents are investor-friendly—not all agents are. If you establish real trust with your agent, ideally he or she will set you up as an unlicensed assistant. This gets you your own login identification at a cost of only around $100 per year. Many investors become agents, in fact, solely for the MLS access. I think it's easier just to become an unlicensed assistant and to pay that person back with loyalty. Whenever you buy a listed property or sell a house retail, use your agent.

ACCOUNTANT

Choose an accountant who specializes in real estate investors. There are endless tax laws and they change each year, so if you don't choose someone who specializes in real estate, you could be leaving thousands of dollars, or tens of thousands, in deductions on the table. This was another very expensive lesson for me. Ask around at your real estate investor group, and interview possible accountants just as you would new employees.

BOARD OF DIRECTORS

Okay, this isn't a literal board of directors like the ones steering Apple or Dow Chemical, but it's incredibly helpful for your growing business to have a group of three to five people you trust. Cultivate this handful of advisors from among the professionals you meet at your local investors group meetings. Some of the people you take to lunch early on to pick their brains about the business might later sit on your "board." The people on my board of directors have all been investing for at least forty years. That's a lot of experience and expertise. Once you've assembled your board, meet quarterly, or at least twice a year, to go over your plans and discuss problems or challenges. What seems like a major challenge to you will often become a minor problem when presented to people with years of experience, since they probably have faced similar challenges in their own careers. I have made some life-changing decisions at these meetings.

CHAPTER 13

RIDING THE REAL ESTATE ROLLER COASTER

I hope that I have given you a realistic view of real estate investing up to this point. My systems are not complicated. If you learn them and work hard, you will succeed, but you also, inevitably, will have ups and downs. It's vital that you understand this as you're learning the ropes, or you can easily get discouraged and quit. Entering this business means riding a roller coaster of emotions, especially early on, and you want to be prepared for the highs and lows and to realize that they're perfectly normal. I wish I'd known about the natural transitions all investors experience before I started investing. Unfortunately, I didn't learn about them until my career was well under way, when I attended an Entrepreneurs' Organization meeting. The speaker, Cameron Herold, detailed the roller-coaster ride that all entrepreneurs—not just real estate investors—face, in his book *Double Double: How to Double Your Revenue and Profit in 3 Years or Less.* His take is fascinating and true to my experience, so I've adapted the stages he explores to real estate investing.

I will examine the stages so that you can identify them when they appear—and believe me, they will appear. Because I've lived through them, I will also advise you on what you should and shouldn't do in each stage.

STAGE 1: UNINFORMED OPTIMISM

This stage feels like getting strapped into your seat on a brand new roller coaster. You're excited, brimming with enthusiasm, and a little nervous because you don't know what to expect. This generally takes place when you meet someone who tells you about real estate investing or attend an investing seminar. As you decide to try it, you tend to view the world through rose-colored glasses. No more 5-Hour Energy drinks for you. You're up early and thrilled to face each day. It's only a matter of time, you think, until you'll realize all of your dreams. There's nothing wrong with this attitude—it's actually a necessary part of getting the ball rolling (this was how I felt formulating the McDonald's Plan I described in chapter 1). But it's important to understand that this is a part of the learning curve so that you're not too disappointed when this stage passes.

In Stage 1, DO

- engage in guerrilla marketing;
- build your investor list;
- assemble your power team (more on this shortly);
- talk to motivated sellers;
- make offers on houses;
- secure private money; and
- attend real estate investor meetings.

You will excel at these things because your enthusiasm and excitement are contagious. People will want to be near you, investors will want to buy from you, and lenders will want to lend to you.

In Stage 1, DON'T

- make long-term decisions or investments (no new offices or cars, for example);

- hire employees;

- sign advertising contracts;

- budget; and

- buy rentals.

The downside of seeing rainbows everywhere is that anyone can sell you anything in this stage—a Ferrari, a secretary, or a long-term billboard contract. You are putty in their hands. If you try to make a budget, it will be way off. If you buy rentals, the decisions will be based on emotions, not numbers. Be cautious in this stage, where long-term damage can be done.

TRANSITION CURVE

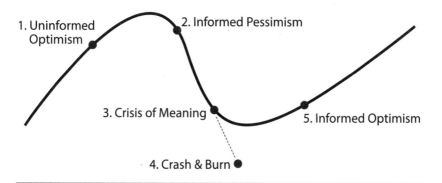

1. Uninformed Optimism

2. Informed Pessimism

3. Crisis of Meaning

4. Crash & Burn

5. Informed Optimism

STAGE 2: INFORMED PESSIMISM

You've gotten to the top of the roller coaster in this stage and can see the drop below. You're wiser and more realistic, and you have a little more information, but this makes you nervous. Beware of the investors' disease we call "paralysis of analysis." This malady makes you go over deals a thousand times—and always find a reason to pull back. Many real estate investors never get out of stage 2. This is when you start to wonder, *Was this really a good idea? Who am I to be a real estate investor? This is harder work than I thought.* Optimism fades.

In Stage 2, DO

- continue guerrilla marketing;

- talk to salesman about other marketing: TV, radio, billboards, etc.;

- make a budget; and

- start looking for rentals.

This is a good time to look into the things you avoided in stage 1 because you're starting to realize how your money will flow and that investing might not be as glamorous as you first thought.

In Stage 2, DON'T

- talk to new private lenders and

- talk directly to new investors on your list (add them, just don't sell to them for now).

I advise you to avoid new lenders and investors in this stage because your lack of confidence will show. No matter what you say, you'll leave them thinking that something is off with you. You won't secure a new lender at this time, so do not burn through the prospects. You won't sell a new investor on a deal here, either, because you haven't truly sold yourself. Emailing your investor list works better at this stage than calling your top buyers.

STAGE 3: CRISIS OF MEANING

You are heading down the roller coaster at full speed, gasping, with heart in mouth. Whoa! Everything you do seems to fall apart. Every deal has new challenges. You think you're the first investor to face each challenge, and you are terrified to get up in the morning. Maybe your brother-in-law was right, with his horror stories about investing. Maybe you can't cut it. You want to call it a day by noon and find someplace quiet to cry.

In Stage 3, DO

- reach out to supportive friends and family;

- work out, run, exercise in some way (key to staying sane and coping);

- clean your desk and car (organization gives you a feeling of control);

- listen to motivational CDs (think Anthony Robbins, not real estate);

- make lists—of both daily tasks and solutions to current challenges;

- talk to older investors, guys with fifty to a hundred rentals who stick around because they love the game;

- read non–real estate business books, success stories to motivate you;

- clarify what you've done right and wrong so far; plan what you'll do differently;

- cut away all anchors—bad deals, burdensome monthly commitments, etc.; and

- get a coach—an objective, professional outsider, to help you move forward.

This is a prime place to quit if you don't remember that this stage is perfectly natural and that we've all been through it. Don't keep things bottled up. Share your worries with the friends and family members who are supportive. Seek out motivation and positive energy where you can—in books, on CDs, from older successful investors, at the gym. Try to get organized and take small steps to getting back on track.

In Stage 3, DON'T

- go back to the negative friends you dropped when you started investing;

- try to handle everything by yourself—share, tough as that might be;

- hang around others with the same problems—they'll bring you down; and

- learn new techniques—gurus make them seem easy, which makes you feel worse.

You will get to know yourself well in this stage. You might realize that this is not the life for you, and that's okay. Real estate investing is tough and not for everyone. If I'm taking the wind out of your sails on the journey to real estate wealth, I apologize, but I'd rather prepare you for the potential downside in advance than have you discover it the hard way. You are at a serious dip in the roller coaster, and every day, you'll face the decision of whether to get off the ride or stay on, hoping to figure things out and begin a new ascent.

STAGE 4: CRASH AND BURN (OPTIONAL)

If you haven't hung on tight and persevered through stage 3, the wheels will come off your car in this stage, the one I'm trying to help you avoid. Stage 4 probably means foreclosure or bankruptcy. You're looking for a way out of the business and becoming one of those motivated sellers you started out courting. Here, you might become fodder for the next gung-ho real estate investor who's still in Stage 1.

In Stage 4, DO

- make as graceful an exit as you can;

- seek experienced investors' advice (many have navigated foreclosure, bankruptcy, etc. and have tips);

- explore options with lenders and creditors (many are more flexible than you think);

- remember, the goal is freedom, not money, and there are other ways to get it; and

- keep your spirits up—continue reaching out to supportive family and friends.

Look back at the start of this book and consider the number of businesses I tried—landscaping, limousines, tanning salons, bars, etc.—before I discovered the niche that was right for me. I have done very well in real estate—it's a game I love—but after running a tanning salon, I quickly decided that I wasn't suited to that business. Bars, I discovered as I ran several, aren't my thing either, and in fact, neither is being a traditional landlord. The goal was never real estate, or even money, but freedom. Try other paths, and you'll eventually find it. "Fail" is a verb, not a noun. It is something that happened and not who you are. You will now feel relief. Take this time to mend relationships that your stress might have affected.

In Stage 4, DON'T

- burn anyone—buyers, lenders, partners, etc.;

- consider yourself a failure—a business failed, not you; and

- think real estate was your only option.

I've emphasized throughout this book how important trust and reputation are—they were your most important tools in entering real estate investing. Don't abandon them because you're exiting it. Communicate with lenders, partners, clients, and loved ones, and be honest about your situation if you need to get out. No one will be happy about your business tanking, certainly not if it means they're losing money or opportunities, but they will likely be more understanding than you think.

STAGE 5: INFORMED OPTIMISM

If you've made it here and avoided stage 4, you have grasped the reality of being a real estate investor and can have a long, profitable career. This does not mean you have passed the last drop in the roller-coaster ride—there will be plenty of others—but the next time one appears, you'll know you can handle it. You are once again calm and optimistic, but your optimism is mixed with reality and grounded.

In Stage 5, DO

- continue buying rentals—and paying them off as soon as possible;

- continue developing and maintaining your buyers list / contacts;

- continue learning: books, seminars, online courses, etc.;

- maintain perspective and think long term; and

- live within your means.

Remember the things that got you to this point, and don't stop doing them. Remember the mistakes you made, too. Given your current knowledge base, what would you do differently? Keep honing your methods, learning, and refining. Thinking you've got it all figured out leads to disaster. Make new contacts, take new courses, read more books. Always be learning.

In Stage 5, DON'T

- get overly confident;

- lose touch with the market after choice buyers refuse a deal;

- outspend your earnings; and

- overleverage yourself.

Your hope and motivation return in this stage. This business is fun again, and you recall why you got into it in the first place. Remember my lessons from early in the book, though. Earning forty grand a month is meaningless if you're spending forty-one. Live within your means. No debt is good debt, so always keep it to a minimum and pay it off as quickly as you can. Don't forget those heart-wrenching dips in the roller coaster either. You'll see more of them—be prepared mentally, emotionally, and financially. This isn't an amusement park. You'll be riding this roller coaster for life, so sit back and enjoy the ride!

 CONCLUSION

YOU ARE A REAL
ESTATE INVESTOR

I started this book by talking about my own experiences partly to explain how my investing philosophy evolved and partly to demonstrate in concrete terms the roller-coaster ride I detailed in the last chapter. I don't want to discourage anyone from investing, only to let new investors know that they will sometimes get discouraged.

I certainly did.

Remember chapter 1, when I described the housing crash of 2007 and how I lost fifty houses to foreclosure and millions in equity? It's hard to imagine a bigger dip on the roller coaster. That one almost sent me packing. At the time, I started talking to friends and associates about other career options. I'd become used to a certain lifestyle though, and short of becoming a surgeon, I didn't see how I could switch gears, do something satisfying, and pull in the same sort of cash.

I picked myself up, dusted myself off, and found a way to make it work. If you want to succeed as an investor, you'll have to do the same thing multiple times while you learn the ropes and build your income stream. If you keep moving forward and don't quit, you will eventually succeed.

All those stories from the first chapter serve another purpose, too. I dropped out of high school, joined the army, and then tried literally dozens of businesses before settling on real estate. Once I focused on housing, I did all sorts of things wrong (see the "McDonald's Plan," massive debt, maintenance headaches, etc.). I did not go to school for this, and I did not have a mentor. I picked up info and techniques wherever I could—from books, seminars, and random investors—but most of my education came from trial and error. Yes, I now travel at least twelve weeks a year, and I'll decide tomorrow whether to hit the office or the pool, but that freedom didn't come overnight. No one had a steeper learning curve than I did. Maybe the most important lesson to draw from chapter 1 is that if I can succeed as a real estate investor, so can you.

Simply getting to the last page of this book puts you miles ahead of where I started out. I read many helpful real estate books while learning this business, but I never had one that offered a thorough overview of investment strategies, practical steps for getting started, and nitty-gritty tips for the hidden parts of the process, such as following up with sellers, taking people to lunch, navigating calls, etc. I wrote this book because I wish I'd had one like it when I began investing.

The various techniques I've presented here will be helpful, but learning them is the easy part. They can seem overwhelming at first, which is why I recommend focusing on doing one thing each day to move closer to your goal: *On Sunday I will read the entire real estate section. On Monday I will order business cards. On Tuesday I will have lunch with that investor I met at my local club. On Wednesday I will buy a new real estate book . . .* Remember, the process early on is all about marketing for leads, and the sooner you work on that, the better.

Finding a mentor—something I wish I'd known to do—will help you learn faster, earn faster, and avoid pitfalls.

If you're determined, all that will work itself out. The hard part of this process, believe it or not, is making the decision to invest and believing that you truly are an investor. No one wants to do deals with someone who's considering becoming an investor. You must think of yourself as an investor now. In fact, I start my seminars by making students repeat out loud after me: *I am a real estate investor!*

Did you say it? Well, say it again. Louder. Okay, now repeat it with conviction every morning when you get out of bed.

Congratulations, you are a real estate investor. Good luck!

REPAIR ANALYSIS WORKSHEET

Address: _____ City: _____ State: _____ Zip: _____

Date: _____ Owner(s)/Trustee: _____ Phone: _____

	Comp 1	Comp 2	Comp 3	Comp 4	Comp 5	Comp 6
House #						
Street						
Sq Ft						
Year Blt						
Sold For						
Gar Con						
Exterior						
Adj $ Sq Ft Value						
SUBJECT PROPERTY	SF:	Yr Blt:	Bed:	Bath:	Gar:	Carport:
	Amenity:				Pool:	Hot Tub:

ANY SERIOUS ISSUE IS SUFFICIENT REASON TO STOP NOW.
THERE ARE ALWAYS OTHER HOUSES!

DEMO/SITE PREP:
- ☐ Landscaping   ☐ Mold   ☐ Permits
- ☐ Pest Control   ☐ Asbestos
Clean Up: Debris Removal: _____ x Pick-Up ($100.00)
                          _____ x Dumpster ($400.00)

FOUNDATION
- ☐ CP&B ($7.00/sq) or _____ x Piers ($350-6ft)   ☐ Post Pier & Beam ($2.00/sq)
- ☐ Slab ($7.00/sq) or _____ x Piers ($350-8ft)   ☐ w/ Basement
- ☐ Thru-Fl Post * w/ 4-12" Crawl Space ($4.00/sq)

FLOORING:
☐ Replace ($2.50/sqft)   ☐ Replace with Ceramic Tile ($4.00/sqft)
Estimate: _____

EXTERIOR:
☐ Gutter (incl. Downspout): _____ x ($4.50/LF)
☐ Replace Vinyl Siding ($4.50/sf Living Area)

ROOFING:
☐ 3-tab ($1.60/sq)   ☐ Dimensional ($2.00/sq) ☐ Re-Deck ($1.20/sq)
☐ Tear-Offs (.30/layer)   ☐ High Pitch & 2-Story Houses w/ a 6/12 Pitch add (.50/sq)
☐ Hot Tar ($1.75/sq)

DOORS:
House: _____ x Int. Door ($100)   _____ x Ext. Door ($200) _____ x Door Jamb ($105)
_____ x Patio Door ($500) _____ x Patio Glass Replace ($150)
Garage: ☐ Single ($350)   ☐ Double ($750)

WINDOWS:
Metal: _____ x Sm ($175)   _____ x Med ($200)   _____ x Lg ($250)
Glass: _____ x Sm ($20)   _____ x Med ($30)   _____ x Lg ($40)
Wood: _____ x Sm ($275)   _____ x Med ($300)   _____ x Lg ($350)

CARPENTRY:
_____ x Soffit ($20/LF)   _____ x Trim ($1.70/LF)
Drywall: _____ x Room ($450)   ☐ House ($3.00/sqft)

PAINT:
☐ Inside ($1.25/sqft)   ☐ Int Door (.25/sq)   ☐ Retex Ceiling (.70/sq)
☐ Retex Walls (.70/sq)   ☐ Wood Win (.30/sq)
Oustide: ☐ Brick ($1.25/sqft)   ☐ Frame ($1.70/sqft)
☐ Siding ($1.50/sqft)   ☐ Stucco ($1.50/sqft)   ☐ Tile Roof Paint ($1.00/sqft)

KITCHEN:
Cabinets: _____ x ($100/LF)   Countertops: _____ x ($30/LF)
☐ Refrig ($500)   ☐ Range ($450)   ☐ Stovetop ($250)
☐ DW ($350)   ☐ Hood ($150)

PLUMBING:
☐ Replace all pipes ($2.005/sqft)   ☐ Hot Water ($400)   ☐ Kitchen Sink ($175)
Toilet: _____ x ($120)   ☐ Vanity ($225)
☐ Sm Tile ($800)   ☐ Lg Tile ($1000)   ☐ Tile Pan ($750)
☐ Tile Stall ($1100)   ☐ Tub ($450)

HEATING/AC:
☐ Replace All ($3.00/sqft)   ☐ Reuse Ducts ($2.50/sqft)   ☐ Clean & Service ($250)
Estimate: _____

ELECTRICAL:
☐ Rewire ($2.50/sqft)   ☐ Service Upgrade ($1300)
_____ x Light Fixtures ($30)   _____ x Ceiling Fans ($90)

APPENDIX B

BASIC CONTRACT

PROPERTY PURCHASE AGREEMENT

THIS PURCHASE AGREEMENT is made this _____ day of _____, 20____,

between **and/or assigns** (Buyer),, and _____ (Seller);

PURCHASE PRICE: Buyer agrees to buy and the Seller agrees to sell for the sum of

_____Dollars

($_____),payable to Seller at settlement in cash or by cashier's or

certified check or wired funds all that certain piece, parcel or lot of land (the Property)

described as follows, to-wit:

* *

ALSO INCLUDING:

All appliances, window and wall treatments, fixtures, including but not limited to the following,

and all personal property left by the seller will become the property of the buyer.

Refrigerator, stove, oven, dishwasher, washer, drier, _____

_____

The Purchase Price to be paid as follows:

$_____ CASH DUE AT CLOSING.
$_____ CONVENTIONAL LOAN TO BE OBTAINED BY BUYERS.
$_____ LOAN FROM SELLER TO BE IN THE FORM OF A SECOND DEED OF
TRUST NOTE, TO BE AMORTIZED OVER 30 YEARS AT THE INTEREST RATE OF
_____ % PER ANNUM, WITH A BALLOON PAYMENT DUE IN 5 YEARS.

Purchase Agreement   Page 1 of 5

_____/_____   _____/_____

Initials of Buyer(s)   Initials of Seller(s)

1. SETTLEMENT: Settlement to be on or before _____, or as soon thereafter as possible allowing reasonable time to process the specified loan and to correct any defects reported by a title examiner (the Settlement Date). Buyer agrees to promptly provide such documentation as lender may require to process and complete the specified financing. However, if through no fault of the Seller, settlement has not occurred within thirty (30) days of the above stated Settlement Date, the Seller at his option may declare this Purchase Agreement null and void by written notice of his intention to do so to Buyer. Nothing contained herein shall be construed to limit in any way any other legal remedy or right Seller may have for Buyer's failure to close on or before Settlement Date or at any time thereafter.

2. POSSESSION: Seller shall deliver to Buyer possession of the Property in its present or required condition at settlement.

3. LOAN APPLICATION: Buyer agrees to apply for the specified financing within five (5) working days of Purchase Agreement acceptance, and to do promptly, diligently, and in good faith, everything necessary to obtain said loan or lender approval for assumption of existing loan(s). If such loan or approval is not obtainable by the Settlement Date, through no fault of the Buyer, for any reason (other than Buyer's failure to have available for settlement the cash required by this Purchase Agreement except as noted herein), all parties hereto shall execute the appropriate release agreement and all parties shall then be released from any further liability hereunder and the earnest money deposit shall be returned to Buyer, excepting out-of-pocket expenses.

4. SETTLEMENT EXPENSES: Seller shall pay all expenses of Deed preparation, the grantor's tax on said Deed, and all expenses, if any, for removal of title defects and those miscellaneous fees charged by lender for the specified financing which, by law, the Buyer is not permitted to pay. Except as otherwise stated below, Buyer agrees to pay appropriate funding fees and mortgage insurance fees in cash at closing unless they are financed, and Buyer shall pay all other expenses when required, including without limitation cost of preparing deed(s) of trust and costs of recording all documents.

5. ESCROW, CLOSING AND SETTLEMENT SERVICE GUIDELINES: The Virginia State Bar issues guidelines to help settlement agents avoid and prevent the unauthorized practice of law in connection with furnishing escrow, settlement or closing services. As a party to a real estate transaction, you are entitled to receive a copy of these guidelines from your settlement agent, upon request, in accordance with the provisions of the consumer real estate settlement protection act.

6. CHOICE OF SETTLEMENT AGENT: Settlement agent for both sides of the transaction will be_____. The settlement agent's role in closing your transaction involves the coordination of numerous administrative and clerical functions relating to the collection of documents and the collection and disbursement of funds required carrying out the terms of this contract between the parties. If part of the purchase price is financed, your lender will instruct the settlement agent as to the signing and recording of the loan documents and the distribution of legal advice to

Purchase Agreement   Page 2 of 5

_____/_____   _____/_____

Initials of Buyer(s)   Initials of Seller(s)

any party of the transaction except a settlement agent who is engaged in the private practice of law in Virginia and who has been retained or engaged by a party to the transaction for the purpose of providing legal services to that party.

7. SPECIAL PROVISIONS AND DISCLOSURES: (Seller to initial statements below.)
_____ Buyer is a professional homebuyer and buys below market value for a profit.
_____ Seller to provide buyer access to property prior to closing through a lock box
        placed on property at the time this contract is signed.
_____ **SELLER ACKNOWLEDGES THAT THIS IS A CONTRACT FOR THE SALE OF THEIR REAL ESTATE AND THERE HAS BEEN NO REPRESENTATION, EITHER WRITTEN OR ORAL, THAT GIVES THE SELLER THE RIGHT TO BUY THE PROPERTY BACK FROM THE PURCHASER.**

8. TERMINATION OPTION: For nominal consideration, the receipt of which is hereby acknowledged by Seller, and Buyer's agreement to pay Seller $10.00 (Option Fee) within 2 days after the effective date of this contract, the Seller grants Buyer the unrestricted right to terminate this contract by giving notice of termination to Seller within 60 days after the effective date of this contract. If no dollar amount is stated as the Option Fee or if Buyer fails to pay the Option Fee within the time prescribed, this paragraph will not be a part of this contract and Buyer shall not have the unrestricted right to terminate this contract. If Buyer gives notice of termination within the time prescribed, the Option Fee will not be refunded; however, any earnest money will be refunded to Buyer. The Option Fee will be credited to the Sales Price at closing.

9. DEED AND TITLE: Seller agrees to convey the Property by General Warranty Deed from owner of record, with the usual English Covenants of Title, subject to any easements and restrictions of record thereon not adversely affecting marketability of title. Title to the Property shall be free and clear of all liens, tenancies and encumbrances of every kind except those stated herein.

10. PRORATIONS: All taxes, insurance, rents, interest, fuel oil, and appropriate condominium or POA fees and reserves are to be prorated as of the Settlement Date.

11. ATTORNEY'S FEES: The prevailing party in any legal proceeding related to this contract is entitled to recover reasonable attorney's fees and all costs of such proceedings incurred by the prevailing party.

12. ASSIGNABILITY: This Purchase Agreement may be assigned by Buyer without the written consent of the Seller.

13. CONTINGENCIES: This Purchase Agreement shall be contingent upon the following conditions:

        Termite Certification and an acceptable Home Inspection, to be completed by buyer.

Purchase Agreement   Page 3 of 5

_____/_____   _____/_____

Initials of Buyer(s)   Initials of Seller(s)

_____
_____
_____

_____
_____
_____

14. CONDITION OF PROPERTY:
   a. ACCESS, INSPECTIONS, AND UTILITIES: Seller shall permit Buyer and Buyer's agents access to the Property through a lock box placed on the property by buyer. Buyer may have the Property inspected by inspectors selected by Buyer. Seller at Seller's expense shall turn on existing utilities for inspections.

   b. RESIDENTIAL PROPERTY DISCLAIMER STATEMENT
      X   Buyer has received the Notice.
   c. SELLER'S DISCLOSURE OF LEAD –BASED PAINT AND LEAD-BASED PAINT HAZARDS is required by Federal law for a residential dwelling constructed prior to 1978.
   d. ACCEPTANCE OF PROPERTY CONDITION: Buyer accepts the Property in its present condition; provided Seller, at Seller's expense, shall complete the following specific   repairs   and   treatments:

   _____

   _____.

   e.   LENDER REQUIRED REPAIRS AND TREATMENTS: Unless otherwise agreed in writing, neither party is obligated to pay for lender required repairs, which includes treatment for wood destroying insects. If the parties do not agree to pay for the lender required repairs or treatments, this contract will terminate and the earnest money will be refunded to Buyer.   If the cost of lender required repairs and treatments exceeds 5% of the Sales Price, Buyer may terminate this contract and the earnest money will be refunded to Buyer.

15. DELIVERY OF PROPERTY Seller agrees to deliver the Property on the Settlement Date or upon possession, whichever event shall first occur, in substantially the same condition as of the date of this Agreement, free of personal property, insect infestation, debris and trash. Seller assumes, until settlement, all risk of loss or damage to the Property by fire, windstorm, casualty or other hazards. Seller shall complete all inspections, repairs or replacements required by lender or any governmental agency or agencies in order to (i) obtain financing,

Purchase Agreement   Page 4 of 5

_____/_____   _____/_____

Initials of Buyer(s)   Initials of Seller(s)

and (ii) permit occupancy of the Property by Buyer, NOT TO EXCEED 1% OF THE PURCHASE PRICE except as follows:

_____

Buyer represents that Buyer has inspected the Property as of the date of this Purchase Agreement, and, subject to the inspections in Paragraph 10 and 13, accepts the Property "as is".

16. WALK THROUGH: Seller warrants that all plumbing, electric, heating and air conditioning systems, and all equipment and appliances which convey with the Property, will be in working order on the Settlement Date or upon possession, whichever occurs first, and Buyer reserves the right to make a "walk through" inspection to determine their working order. The Buyer acknowledges that he has not relied upon any statements or representations by the undersigned Seller which are not herein expressed. All utilities necessary for the "walk through" inspection shall be provided by SELLER.

17 WOOD DESTROYING INSECTS/MOISTURE: Seller shall provide an approved VA/FHA wood destroying insect report from a licensed pest control operator prior to Settlement Date showing the Property's principal dwelling and garage to be free of visible wood destroying insect infestation with no visible unrepaired damage from said infestation. Said report shall also include those readily accessible areas of the foundation and understructure including crawl space, sills, joists, sub flooring and substructure support timbers to be free of standing water and/or visible moisture damage. Cost of inspection and required treatment and repairs shall be paid by Seller.

THIS IS A LEGALLY BINDING AGREEMENT.
IF NOT UNDERSTOOD, SEEK LEGAL ADVICE

BUYER By: _____
                                    (Signature)   **(DATE)**

SELLER:

By: _____   _____
          (Signature)   **(DATE)**   **(Signature)**   **(DATE)**

        _____   _____
                    (SSN)   **(SSN)**

_____
    (Primary Mortgage Company; Account #, & Phone Number)

_____
    (Secondary Mortgage Company; Account #, & Phone Number)

Purchase Agreement   Page 5 of 5

_____/_____   _____/_____

Initials of Buyer(s)   Initials of Seller(s)

OPTION FEE RECEIPT

Receipt of $_____ (Option Fee) in the form of _____
Was received.

_____   _____/_____/_____
              Seller   Date

CONTRACT AND EARNEST MONEY RECEIPT

Receipt of ___Contract and ___$_____ Earnest Money in the form of
_____ is acknowledged.

_____   _____/_____/_____
           Escrow Agent   Date

By: _____   _____
           Signature   E-Mail Address

_____   _____
           Address   Phone

_____   _____
             City   State, Zip

                                             _____
                                                             Fax

Purchase Agreement   Page 6 of 5

_____/_____   _____/_____

Initials of Buyer(s)   Initials of Seller(s)

APPENDIX C

ASSIGNMENT FORM

Assignment of Contract

The undersigned Assignor, having executed a contract dated _____

between_____, Contractor and_ _____

Contractee concerning the property described as:___ _____, hereby

assigns all rights to said contract to_____ _ __

_____

("Assignee") in exchange for compensation in the amount of _____

Assignee agrees to fulfill all terms, conditions, and contingencies of said Contract and to

perform as required in good faith and within any time periods established by said

Contract this _____ day of _____, 20_____.

This assignment must be closed by _____)_____. Time is of the essence.

This assignment will automatically be voided if not closed by _____.

_____ Owner of _____., will act as consultant to this

contract, and will work with assignee and seller to see the contract through to closing.

Assignee Phone Number: _____ (W) _____(C)

Assignee Address: _____

_____   _____

Assignor   Witness

_____   _____

Assignee   Witness